THE ZINGARA ART OF
DIVINATION

Some Other Titles From New Falcon Publications

Aha! The Sevenfold Mystery of the Ineffable Love   –Aleister Crowley
An Insider's Guide to Robert Anton Wilson   –Eric Wagner
Bio-Etheric Healing   –Trudy Lanitis
Undoing Yourself With Energized Meditation and Other Devices
Secrets of Western Tantra: The Sexuality of the Middle Path
Dogma Daze   –Christopher S. Hyatt, Ph.D.
Rebels & Devils; The Psychology of Liberation–Edited by Christopher S. Hyatt, Ph.D.
Aleister Crowley's Illustrated Goetia, Sex Magic, Tantra & Tarot:
The Way of the Secret Lover, Taboo: Sex, Religion & Magick
    Christopher S. Hyatt, Ph.D., and DuQuette
Pacts With The Devil, Urban Voodoo: A Beginner's Guide to Afro-Caribbean Magic
    –Jason Black and Christopher S. Hyatt, Ph.D.
The Psychopath's Bible   –Christopher S. Hyatt, Ph.D., and Jack Willis
Ask Baba Lon   –Lon Milo DuQuette
Aleister Crowley and the Treasure House of Images
    –J.F.C. Fuller, Aleister Crowley, Lon Milo DuQuette and Nancy Wasserman
Enochian Sex Magic and How To Workbook
    –Aleister Crowley, Lon Milo DuQuette and Christopher S. Hyatt, Ph.D.
Enochian World of Aleister Crowley   –DuQuette and Aleister Crowley
Info-Psychology, Neuropolitique, The Game of Life, What Does WoMan Want?
    –Timothy Leary, Ph.D.
Nonlocal Nature: The Eight Circuits of Consciousness   –James A. Heffernan
on What is   –Ja Wallin
Rebellion, Revolution and Religiousness   –Osho
Reichian Therapy: A Practical Guide for Home Use   –Dr. Jack Willis
Shaping Formless Fire, Seizing Power, Taking Power,
The Magick in the Music and Other Essays   –Stephen Mace
The Illuminati Conspiracy: The Sapiens System   –Donald Holmes, M.D.
The Secret Inner Order Rituals of the Golden Dawn   –Pat Zalewski
The Why, Who, and What of Existence   Vlad Korbel
Steamo Goes to Havana, The Social Epidemic of Child Abuse
    Michael Miller, M.Ed., M.S., Ph.D.
Woman's Orgasm: A Guide to Sexual Satisfaction
    –Benjamin Graber, M.D., and Georgia Kline-Graber, R.N.

Other Titles by J. Marvin Spiegelman, Ph.D.

A Modern Jew in Search of Soul
Buddhism and Jungian Psychology
Catholicism and Jungian Psychology
Hinduism and Jungian Psychology
Mysticism, Psychology and Oedipus - A Small Gem
Protestanism and Jungian Psychology
Psychotherapy and Religion at the Millennium and Beyond
Psychotherapy as a Mutual Process
Reich, Jung, Regardie & Me - The Unhealed Healer
Rider, Haggard, Henry Miller & I - The Unpublished Writer
Sufism, Islam and Jungian Psychology
The Knight - A Small Gem
The Nymphomaniac
The Quest - Further Adventures in the Unconscious
The Tree of Life - Paths in Jungian Individuation
The Wisdom of J. Marvin Speigelman Vol. I - Selected Writings
The Wisdom of J. Marvin Speigelman Vol. II - Psychology and Religion

Other Titles by Dr. Israel Regardie

A Garden of Pomegranates
A Practical Guide to Geomantic Divination - A Small Gem
Attract and Use Healing Energy - A Small Gem
Be Yourself - A Guide to Relaxation and Health
Ceremonial Magic
*Dr. Israel Regardie's Definitive Work on Aleister Crowley,
   The Eye In The Triangle*
Healing Energy, Prayer and Relaxation
How To Make and Use Talismans - A Small Gem
Israel Regardie's The Foundations of Practical Magick
My Rosicrucian Adventure
Mysticism, Psychology and Oedipus - A Small Gem
Practical Magick - A Small Gem
Teachers of Fulfillment
The Art and Meaning of Magic - A Small Gem
The Body-Mind Connection, A Path to Well-Being - A Small Gem
The Complete Golden Dawn System of Magic
The Complete Golden Dawn System of Magic Book 1 - Ltd. Edition
The Complete Golden Dawn System of Magic Book 2 - Ltd. Edition
The Complete Golden Dawn System of Magic - The Black Edition
The Eye in the Triangle: An Interpretation of Aleister Crowley
The Golden Dawn Audio CDs, Vol. 1, Vol. 2, and Vol. 3
The Legend of Aleister Crowley
The Magic of Israel Regardie
The Middle Pillar
The Philosopher's Stone
The Portable Complete Golden Dawn System of Magic
The Tree of Life
*The Wisdom of Israel Regardie - Vol. I
   Selected Introductions, Prefaces and Forewords*
*The Wisdom of Israel Regardie - Vol. II
   Selected Essays and Commentaries*
*The Wisdom of Israel Regardie - Vol. III
   Selected Articles, Introductions, Prefaces and Forewords*
What You Should Know About the Golden Dawn
Wilhelm Reich, His Theory And Techniques
Aha! (Dr. Israel Regardie and Aleister Crowley)
Roll Away The Stone/The Herb Dangerous
   (Dr. Israel Regardie and Aleister Crowley)

MANY OF OUR TITLES AVAILABLE ON KINDLE!
Please visit our website at http://www.newfalcon.com

Copyright ©New Falcon Publications 2023

All rights reserved. No part of this book, in part or in whole, may be reproduced, transmitted, or utilized, in any form or by any means, electronic or mechanical, including photocopying, recording, or by any information storage and retrieval system, without permission in writing from the publisher, except for brief quotations in critical articles, books and reviews.

ISBN 13: 978-1-56184-518-7
ISBN 10: 1-56184-518-3

New Falcon Publications First Edition 2023

The paper used in this publication meets the minimum requirements of the American National Standard for Permanence of Paper for Printed Library Materials Z39.48-1984

Printed in USA

NEW FALCON PUBLICATIONS

2046 Hillhurst Avenue
Los Angeles, CA 90027
www.newfalcon.com
email: info@newfalcon.com

THE ZINGARA ART OF DIVINATION

A TREATISE ON THE ART OF PREDICTING FUTURE EVENTS

Ana Caldaroni

NEW FALCON PUBLICATIONS
LOS ANGELES, CALIFORNIA, U.S.A.

PREFACE

Loving, as we gypsies do, the meadows and the woods and the flowers, and living far from the haunts of men, it is not to be wondered at that we get nearer to the heart of nature, and have been able to lift the veil from the future and learn a thousand secrets that the dwellers in cities wot not of. It is not easy to convince everybody that there is truth in what we tell them, but it is for the men and women who are open to conviction and are unprejudiced that this little book has been compiled.

I have written down many things that are matters of personal knowledge, and besides these I have consulted numerous ancient manuscripts, and have also added certain deductions from modern sources so that you may enjoy and learn from *The Art of Zingara Divination*.

Ana Caldaroni

TABLE OF CONTENTS

❖❖❖❖❖❖

Preface — vi

CHAPTER 1	The Cabalistic Chart	1
CHAPTER 2	Charms	5
CHAPTER 3	The Fortune in the Tea Cup	17
CHAPTER 4	Fortune Telling by Cards	23
CHAPTER 5	Fortune Telling by Dice	53
CHAPTER 6	Fortune Telling by Dominoes	89
CHAPTER 7	The Meaning of Dreams	99
CHAPTER 8	Lucky and Unlucky Days	101
CHAPTER 9	The Language of Flowers	115
CHAPTER 10	The Meaning of Moles	121
CHAPTER 11	The Moon's Age	131
CHAPTER 12	Omens	135
CHAPTER 13	Weather Omens	157
CHAPTER 14	Written on the Palm	173
CHAPTER 15	Physiognomy	179

A	B	C	D	E	F	G	H	I
1	2	3	4	5	6	7	8	9
K	L	M	N	O	P	Q	R	S
10	20	30	40	50	60	70	80	90
T	U	X	Y	Z	J	V	Hi	Hu
100	200	300	400	500	600	700	800	900

CHAPTER 1

The Cabalistic Chart

An old letter-chart is still used by the gypsies when they tell fortunes from cabalistic characters. It is one of the easiest of all methods of ascertaining what the future has in store. Among soothsayers, however, it is rarely employed; one reason for this being that so many spurious charts have been made, it is next to impossible to stake a reputation upon one. The original chart given here is the identical one by which sages of the past were able to drag aside the curtain and peer into the beyond. It can, therefore, be fully relied upon.

To use the chart, all that is necessary is to select from it the letters that make up the name of the person whose character you are desirous of learning. Add together the figures underneath. The sum total will reveal all you wish by reference to the table that follows. When the sum exceeds the highest number on the chart, the first figure is cut off and the remainder alone used.

It will be noticed that the letter W does not appear in the chart. When W occurs in a name, two V's must be used. The J and V will be found, not in their alphabetical position, but after the Z.

A	B	C	D	E	F	G	H	I
1	2	3	4	5	6	7	8	9
K	L	M	N	O	P	Q	R	S
10	20	30	40	50	60	70	80	90
T	U	X	Y	Z	J	V	Hi	Hu
100	200	300	400	500	600	700	800	900

The Table
1. Passion, ambition, design
2. Destruction, death, catastrophe
3. Religion, destiny, the soul, charms
4. Solidity, wisdom, power
5. The stars, happiness, graces, marriage
6. Perfection, labor
7. Course of life, repose, liberty, perfect happiness
8. Justice, preservation
9. Imperfection, diminution, grief, pain, expectation
10. Success, reason, future happiness
11. Faults, punishment, discord, prevarication
12. Good omen, a town, or city
13. Impiety
14. Sacrifice, purification
15. Piety, self-culture
16. Love, happiness, voluptuousness
17. Misfortune, forgetfulness
18. Hardening of heart, misfortune
19. Folly
20. Austerity, sadness
21. Mystery, wisdom, the creation
22. A scourge, the divine vengeance

23. Ignorance of the doctrines of Christianity
24. A journey
25. Intelligence, a birth
26. Useful work
27. Firmness, courage
28. Love tokens
29. Letters
30. Fame, a wedding
31. Love of glory, virtue
32. Marriage
33. Purity
34. Suffering trouble of mind
35. Health, harmony
36. Genius, vast conception
37. Domestic virtues, conjugal love
38. Imperfection, avarice, envy
39. Praise
40. Fetes, wedding
41. Ignominy
42. A short and unhappy life, the tomb
43. Religious ceremonies, a priest
44. Power, pomp, monarchy
45. Population
46. Fertility
47. Long and happy life
48. Tribunal, judgment, judge
49. Love of money
50. Pardon, liberty
60. Widowhood
70. Initiated, science, the graces
75. The world
77. Pardon, repentance
80. A cure
81. An adept

90.	Blindness, error, affliction
100.	Divine favor
120.	Patriotism, praises
215.	Calamity
300.	Safety, belief, faith, philosophy
318.	Divine messenger
350.	Hope, justice
360.	Home, society
365.	Astronomy
400.	Priest, theology
500.	Holiness
600.	Perfection
666.	A malicious person, machinations, plots, enemies
700.	Strength
800.	Empire
900.	War, combats, struggles
1000.	Mercy
1095.	Taciturnity
1260.	Torments
1390.	Persecution

Example: Suppose the name of Hugh Holmes be taken. Here, according to the Zingari chart:

Hu represents 900; G, 7; H, 8; total, 915.

H represents 8; O, 50; L, 20; M, 30; E, 5' S, 90; total, 203.

Adding together the two totals, 915 and 203, the grand sum is shown as 1118.

Taking away the first figure we have a singular unenviable destiny revealed.

The number 100 tells us that divine favor was at first shown, but 18 tells the story of the fall, hardening of heart, and finally misfortune.

CHAPTER 2

Charms

TO REVEAL YOUR FUTURE HUSBAND

This charm must be used only on the twenty-first of January, known as St. Agnes' day.

You must prepare yourself by a twenty-four hours' fast, touching nothing but pure spring water, beginning at midnight on the twentieth, to the same again on the twenty-first; then go to bed and mind you sleep by yourself and do not mention what you are trying to any one, or it will break the spell; go to rest on your left side, and repeat these lines three times:

St. Agnes, be a friend to me,
In the gift I ask of thee:
Let me this night my husband see–

and you will dream of your future spouse; if you see more than one in your dream, you will wed two or three times, but if you sleep and dream not, you will never marry.

THE MYRTLE CHARM

Another method of having your future husband revealed in a dream is by the myrtle charm, which must be used only on the twenty-fifth of November, St. Catherine's Day.

Let any number of young women, not exceeding seven or less than three, assemble in a room where they are sure to be safe from interlopers; just as the clock strikes eleven at night, take from your bosom a sprig of myrtle, which you must have worn there all day, and fold it up in a bit of tissue paper; then light up a small chafing dish of charcoal, and on it let each maiden throw nine hairs from her head, and a paring of her toe and finger nails; then let each sprinkle a small quantity of myrtle and frankincense in the charcoal, and while the odiferous vapor rises fumigate your myrtle (this plant or tree is consecrated to Venus) with it. Go to bed while the clock is striking twelve, and you will be sure to dream of your future husband, and place the myrtle exactly under your head. Observe, it is no manner of trying this charm if you are not a real virgin, and the myrtle hour of performance must be passed in strict silence.

TO MAKE YOUR LOVER COME

If a maid wishes to see her lover, let her take the following method: Prick the third, or wedding finger of your left hand with a sharp needle (beware of a pin), and with the blood write your own and lover's name on a piece of clean writing paper, in as small a compass as you can, and encircle it with three round rings of the same crimson stream; fold it up, and exactly at the ninth hour of the evening bury it with your own hand in the earth, and tell no one. Your lover will hasten to you as soon as possible, and he will not be able to rest until he sees you, and, if you have quarreled, to make it up. A young man may also try to charm, only, instead of the wedding finger, let him pierce his left thumb.

APPLE PARINGS

On the twenty-eighth of October, which is a double Saint's day, take an apple, pare it whole, and take the paring in your right hand, and, standing in the middle of the room, say the following:

St. Simon and Jude,
On you I intrude,
By this paring I hold to discover,
Without any delay,
To tell me this day,
The first letter of my own true lover.

Turn round three times, and cast the paring over your left shoulder, and it will form the first letter of your future husband's surname; but if the paring breaks into many pieces, so that no letter is discernible, you will never marry. Take the pips of the same apple, put them in spring water, and drink them.

IS THE MARRIAGE DAY NEAR?

To know how soon a person will be married, get a green pea-pod, in which are exactly nine peas, hang it over the door, and then take notice of the next person who comes in who is not the family, and if it proves a bachelor, you will certainly be married within a year.

On any Friday throughout the year take rosemary flowers, bay leaves, thyme and sweet marjoram, of each a handful; dry these, and make them into a fine powder; then take a teaspoon of each sort, mix the powders together; then take twice the quantity of barley flour and make the whole into cake with the milk of a red cow. This cake is not be baked, but wrapped in clean writing paper, and laid under your head any Friday night. If the person dreams of music, she will wed those she desires, and that shortly; if of fire, she will be crossed in love, if of a church, she will die single. If anything is written or the least spot of ink is on the paper, it will not do.

YOUR HUSBAND'S FORTUNE

To know what fortune your future husband will be. Take a walnut, a hazelnut and nutmeg; grate them together, and mix them with butter and sugar, and make them up into small pills, of which exactly nine must be taken on going to bed; and according to her dreams, so will be the state of the person she will marry. If a gentleman, of riches, if a clergyman, of white linen, if a lawyer, of darkness; if a tradesman, off noises and tumults; if a soldier or sailor, of thunder and lightening; if a servant, of rain.

THE UNBORN CHILD

To know if a woman with child will have a girl or boy. Write the proper names of the father and the mother, and of the month she conceived with child, and likewise adding all the numbers of those letters together, divide them by seven; and then if the remainder be even, it will be a girl; if uneven, it will be a boy.

To know if the child new-born shall live or not. Write the proper names of the father and mother, and on the day the child was born, and put to each letter its number, as you did before, and unto the total sum, being collected, together put twenty-five, and then divide the whole by seven; and then, if it be even, the child shall die; but if it be uneven, the child shall live.

MIDSUMMER-DAY CHARM

To know your husband's trade. Exactly at twelve, on Midsummer-day, place a bowl of water in the sun, pour into some boiling pewter as the clock is striking, saying thus:

Here I try a potent spell,
Queen of love, and Juno tell,
In kind union unto me,
What my husband is to be.
This the day, and this the hour,
When it seems you have the power
For to be a maiden's friend,
So, good ladies, condescend.

A tobacco-pipe full is enough. When the pewter is cold, take it out of the water, and drain it dry in a cloth, and you will find the emblems of your future husband's trade quite plain. If more than one, you will marry twice; if confused and no emblems, you will never marry; a coach shows a gentleman for you.

A CHARM FOR DREAMING

When you go to bed, place under your pillow a Common Prayer Book, open at the part of the matrimonial service, in which is printed, "With this ring I thee wed," etc., place on it a key, a ring, a flower and a spring of willow, a small heart cake, a crust of bread, and the following cards, the ten of clubs, nine of hearts, ace of spades, and the ace of diamonds; wrap all these round in a handkerchief of thin gauze or muslin, on getting into bed cross your hands and say:

Luna, every woman's friend,
To me thy goodness condescend;
Let me this night in visions see,
Emblems of my destiny

If you dream of storms, trouble will betide you; if the storm ends in a fine calm, so will your fate; if of a ring, or of the ace of diamonds, marriage; bread, an industrious life; cake, a prosperous life; flowers, joy; willow, treachery in love; spades, death; diamonds, money; clubs, a foreign land; hearts, illegitimate children; keys, that you will rise to great trust and power, and never know want, birds, that you will have many children; geese, that you will marry more than once.

THE FLOWER SPELL

If a young man or woman receives a present of flowers, or a nosegay from their sweethearts, unsolicited (for is asked for, it destroys the influence of the spell), let them keep them in the usual manner in cold water four-and-twenty hours, then shift the water, and let them stand another twenty-four hours, then take them, and immerse the stalks in water nearly boiling, leave them to perish, or drooping, your lover is false; if revived and blooming, you will be happy in your choice.

THE FROG CHARM

Take a healthy, well-grown frog. Place it in a box which has been pierced all over with holes with a stout darning needle or something similar. Then carry it in the evening twilight to a large ant-heap, place it in the midst of the heap, taking care to observe perfect silence.

After the lapse of a week, repair to the ant-heap, take out the box, and open it, when in place of the frog you will find nothing but a skeleton. Take this apart very carefully, and you will soon find among the delicate bones a scale shaped like that of a fish and a hook. You will need them both. The hook you must contrive to fasten in some way or other into the clothes of the person whose affections you wish to obtain, and if he or she has worn it, if it is only for a quarter of a minute, he will be constrained to love you, and will continue to do so.

THE WEDDING RING CHARM

For a girl to ascertain if she will ever marry, borrow a wedding ring from a young married woman–the more recently she has been married the better– and do not tell her, or let her suspect your purpose; wear this ring on the third finger of your left hand at least three hours after sunset before you retire to rest. When you are ready to go to bed, take half a sheet of pure white paper, with no rule marks or anything upon it, lay down the ring on the paper and mark round it so as to make a circle exactly its size; you then write within the circle, "With this ring I hope to wed;" write your name over the top, and your age underneath; fold the paper with a three-cornered love-letter fold, and put it under your pillow so that it will hang about six inches above your face. You will then dream of several men, the one whose appearance pleases you best will be the man. If you dream of women or girls exclusively, you will never marry. Sometimes it may happen that your dream is confused, and you have no clear recollection of it, or perhaps you may not dream at all, in which case you must continue the charm, by keeping the paper under your pillow for three nights; but the ring is not necessary after the first night.

THE NEW MOON

On first seeing the new moon, if you happen to look at it over your right shoulder, you may make a silent wish, and you will realize it. If a girl thus observes the new moon, and desires to see her future husband, she must repeat to herself (so as not to be heard by anyone) the following lines:

*New moon, new–pray let me see
Who my husband is to be;
The color of his hair,
The clothes he is to wear,
And the happy day that he'll wed me!*

If she is to be married that year, she will positively see the man of her choice before the wane of the full moon.

THE BRIDE'S OMEN

If you would have fair weather on your wedding day, you must always faithfully feed the cats. It is true it is a common error when persons think that it forebodes evil when it rains upon the bride in her bridal dress. This is no evil omen, but the contrary. But, above all things, let her be careful not to allow her shoes to get wet.

THE CROW SIGN

If you wish to know how matters will go with you during the year, you must take good heed of the first crow that you see in the spring. If, when you first see it, it is flying, it signifies that you will take a journey that will be longer or shorter, according to the distance which the bird flies before it alights. It may also signify a complete change of abode, perhaps by a wedding. If you first see the bird sitting, you will remain home; if cawing, much that you do not think of will happen to you; if upon one leg, fortune will not smile upon you.

THE RABBIT AUGURY

If, when in the open field, or upon the highroad, a rabbit runs across your path, it signifies that something unpleasant will happen to you.

THE SHEEP AND SWINE TOKEN

If you are going to pay a visit, and you meet with sheep, you will be very welcome; but if you meet with swine, you will be unwelcome.

A CHARM AGAINST NIGHTMARES

If you wish to be secure against the nightmare in your sleep, place your shoes side by side upon the floor, at the foot of the bed, so that the toes will point not toward the bed, but in the contrary direction, as if they were going from it.

THE SPIDER'S WEB

If you are walking with a young man at a time when the so-called gossamer, those snow-white spider's threads, are floating about in the air, and one of these delicate fibrous veils sweeps by, and forms a band between you and him, it is a sign that feelings of a tender nature will some day bind you to each other.

If a thick, long spider's web hangs anywhere from the ceiling, you must sweep it down as soon as possible, for it signifies a suitor, and the one that gets the web will have him.

WHEN AT NEEDLEWORK

If you are sewing upon a new dress, apron, etc., and you accidently prick your finger with the needle so as to bring blood, it is a sign that when you first wear the garment you will receive many kisses.

TOLD BY WAX

Place a good-sized piece of wax in a melting-ladle, and dissolve it over the coals, or over a spirit-lamp into which you have poured a little alcohol. You must then take a vessel full of water (a bowl is best, that is not too deep nor too shallow), and pour into it the wax, and from the various figures which it forms in the water you endeavour to tell your fortune.

A NEW YEAR'S CHARM

This is for us on New Year's Eve. Take four saucers; in one you put a ring, in another a sprig of myrtle, in the third a piece of money, and in the fourth nothing. The individuals composing the company must now walk around the table, blindfolded, one after the other, and choose one of the saucers, which, in the meantime, have been changed as to place. Those among the company who choose the ring will be betrothed in the course of the year' myrtle signifies wedlock, the piece of money wealth, the empty saucer no change of circumstances.

IN THE MIRROR

Another charm for New Year's Eve is performed in this way: Take two candles, go a little before twelve o'clock into an adjoining chamber–no one on any account must follow you–place yourself before the mirror, and exactly as it strikes twelve, call out your own name in full, three times. When the last sound has died away, you will see in the glass your future husband looking over your shoulder.

FORTUNES IN NUTS

Among the witcheries for New Year's Eve is the nut charm. Each person of the company takes a nutshell, and, after lighting a wax taper, places it in the shell. A basin of water is then brought. You now place the nutshells, with the burning tapers in them, in the basin. Some will incline toward each other as they float along, others will repel each other, until, at last, all are extinguished or sunk. What conclusions in reference to the future are to be drawn from the various movements of these tiny magic skiffs your own quick wits will tell you.

ACROSS THE BRIDGE

Take a glass of water, cut a small chip of wood, and lay it crosswise upon the glass, so that it stretches like a bridge, from one end to the opposite one. Then place this glass under your bed. The consequence will be that you will dream during the night that you are walking over a bridge, and that you fall into the water. A gentleman, however, appears and rescues you. This same gentleman, whom you will see very distinctly, be careful to remember, for his is your future husband. A gentleman can make the same experiment, and he will dream the same thing, with the difference only that it is a lady who rescues him, and she is to be his future wife.

"THINK OF ME"

If you wish any person to think of you, pluck a hair from your head, and blow it out into the air toward that quarter of the heavens in which the person lives, while, at the same time, you call out the name of this person three times, at the top of your voice. During this you must be entirely alone, and must have thought intently upon the person for, at least, a quarter of an hour beforehand. At the same instant he will experience a strange unearthly shudder or thrill, and his thoughts will turn irresistibly toward you.

A HALLOWEEN CHARM

One way to read your fortune by the white of an egg is to break a new-laid egg, and, carefully separating the yolk from the white, drop the latter into a large tumbler half full of water; place this, uncovered, in some dry place, and let it remain untouched for four-and-twenty hours, by which time the white of the egg will have formed itself into various figures–rounds, squares, ovals, animals, trees, crosses, etc.,–which are to be interpreted in the same manner as those formed by the coffee grounds. Of course, the more whites there are in the glass, the more figures there will be. This is more often used on Halloween.

CHAPTER 3

The Fortune in the Tea Cup

Nearly everybody has made an attempt to discover the hidden meaning in the grounds left in the tea or coffee cup. The only reliable way to proceed is as follows:

Preliminary: Pour the grounds of coffee or tea into a white cup, shake them well about in it, so that their particles may cover the surface of the whole cup; then reverse it into the saucer, that all the superfluous parts may be drained, and the figures required for fortune-telling be formed.

The person who acts as the fortune teller must always bend his or her thoughts upon him or her who is to have their fortune told. It is not to be expected that upon taking up the cup the figures will be accurately represent as they are in reality, but it will be quite sufficient if they bear some resemblance to any of the emblems; and the more fertile the fancy is of the person that inspects the cup the more he or she will discover in it.

In other respects, every one who takes a pleasure in this amusement must be a judge under what circumstances he or she is to make changes in point of time–speaking, just as it suits, in the present, the past, or the future; in the same manner, this ingenuity ought to direct the when to speak more or less pointedly with regard to sex.

The Roads or separate lines, indicate ways; if they are covered with clouds, and, consequently, in the thick, they are said to be infallible marks, either of many great or future reverses. But if they appear in the clear and serene, are the surest token of some fortunate change near at hand; encompassed with many points or dots, they signify either a gain of money, or long life.

The Ring signifies marriage; if a letter is near it, it denotes to the person that has their fortune told the initial of the name of the party to be married. If the ring is in the clear; it portends happy and lucrative friendship; if surrounded with clouds, the contrary. But if the ring appear at the bottom of the cup, forebodes the probability of a separation.

The Leaf of Clover is, as well here in common life, a lucky sign. Its different position in the cup alone makes the difference; because, if it be on the top, it shows that the good fortune is not far distant; but it is subject to delay if it be in the middle or at the bottom. Should clouds surround it, it shows that many disagreeables will attend the good fortune; in the clear, it prognosticates serene and undisturbed happiness.

The Anchor. The emblem of hope and commerce, implies successful business carried on by water and by land, if on the bottom of the cup; at the top and in the clear part, it shows constant love and fidelity; but in thick and cloudy parts, it denotes inconstancy.

The Serpent, always the emblem of falsehood and enmity, is likewise here a general sign of an enemy. On the top or in the middle of the cup, it promises to the consulting party that by his always acting properly, his enemies will not be able to triumph over him; if in the thick or cloudy part, he must watch his temper and actions very carefully to prevent great troubles.

The Coffin, the emblem of death, prognosticates the same thing here, or at least a long and tedious illness, if it be in the thick or turbid. In the clear, it denotes long life; if in the thick, at the top of the cup, it signifies a considerable estate likely to be made by cautious industry.

The Dog, being at all times the emblem of fidelity or envy, has a two-fold meaning here. At the top, in the clear, it signifies true and faithful friends; if the image be surrounded with clouds and dashes, it shows that some whom you take for your friends are not to be depended on; but if the dog be a the bottom of the cup, take much care not to excite any person to envy or jealousy, or you will have to dread the effects of both.

The Lily If this emblem be at the top, or in the middle of the cup, it signifies that the consulting party either has, or will have, a good spouse; if it be at the bottom, it denotes anger. In the clear, the lily further betokens a long and happy life; if clouded, or in the thick, it portends trouble and vexations.

The Cross, in general, predicts adversities; if it be at the top, and in the clear, it indicates that the misfortunes of the party will soon be at any end, or that he will, by careful conduct, easily get over them; but if it appear in the middle, or at the bottom of the thick, the party must expect many severe trials; if it appear with dots, either in clear or thick, it promises recompense for sorrow.

The Clouds If they be more bright than dark, you may expect a good result from your hopes; but if they are black, you may give it up. Surrounded with dots, they imply success in trade, if you are saving, and not too venturesome; the brighter they are, the greater will be your happiness.

The Sun, is an emblem of the greatest luck and happiness, if in the clear; but in the thick, it denotes a great degree of illness; surrounded by dots and dashes, it foretells that, without much circumspection, an alteration will soon take place.

The Moon If it appears in the clear, it denotes high honors; in the dark or thick parts, it implies disappointment and sadness, which will, however, pass without great prejudice. But if it be at the bottom of the cup, the consulting party may expect, by industry and prudent conduct, to be very fortunate.

The Star denotes happiness, if in the clear, and at the top of the cup; if clouded, or in the thick, it signifies long life, though exposed to various troubles. If dots are about it, it foretells fortune and respectability. Several dots denote good children; surrounded by dots, it predicts that, without good bringing up, they may cause you grief and vexation.

Mountains If it present only one mountain, it indicates the favor of people of rank; but several of them, especially in the thick, are signs of powerful enemies; in the clear, they signify the contrary or friends in high life.

The Letter Signifies both pleasant and unpleasant news. If this emblem is in the clear part, it denotes the speedy arrival of welcome news; surrounded with dots, it announces the arrival of a remittance of money; but hemmed in by clouds, it forebodes some melancholy or bad tidings, a loss, or some other accident; if it be in the clear, and accompanied by a heart, lovers may expect a favorable letter; but in the thick it denotes the contrary.

The Tree One tree only is indicative of good health; a group of trees in the clear part betokens misfortunes, but which may be avoided by carefulness and industrious habits; several trees, wide apart, promise that your wishes will be accomplished; if they be encompassed by dashes, it is a token that your fortune is in its blossom, and requires only your own care and prudence to bring it to maturity; if the trees be accompanied by dots, it is a sign of riches.

The Child In the clear part, it bespeaks innocent intercourse between the consulter and another person; in the thick part, it signifies crosses in love matters, and requires your utmost care to prevent great expenses; and a family without means of support.

The Woman Signifies much joy in general. If in the clear, this emblem shows very great happiness; but in the thick part, it cautions against jealousy. If dots surround the image, it shows children and wealth.

The Pedestrian Denotes in general a merchant, good business, pleasant news, or the recovery of lost things. It denotes to the female a kind and industrious husband; it also signifies some engagement, and a short journey.

The Rider or Horseman Denotes a letter, good news from abroad, a good situation, or the like; it also foretells that a fortune is to be obtained by care and industry.

The Mouse As this animal lives by stealth, it also is an emblem of theft or robbery; if it be in the clear, it shows that your loss will be easily prevented; but if in the thick, you must use your utmost watchfulness.

The Rose, or Any Other Flower Usually indicates success in science or art by study; if married, good children may be expected, and all the happy fruits, if they have but a good education and good examples.

The Heart If it be in the clear, it signifies future pleasure. It promises joy at receiving some money, if surrounded with dots. If a ring or two hearts be together, it signifies that the party may expect to be married; if a letter is perceptible near it, it shows the initial of the person's name.

The Garden, Wood, or Bush Signifies a large company. In the clear and with leaves, it indicates good friends; in the thick, encompassed with streaks, or if without leaves, it is a token of the caprices of fortune, and warns the consulting party to be cautious whom they take for their friends.

The Rod Predicts differences with people about matters relating to legacies; in the thick, it denotes some affliction, which will require your utmost care to avert.

The Bird in General In the clear, it signifies that the disagreeables and troubles with which you will have to combat will only be surmounted by persevering in doing good; in the thick, it is a sign of good living; also a speedy journey, or voyage, which, if there be dashes, is likely to be to a distance.

Fish in General Imply some lucky event by water, if in the clear, which will either happen to the consultant, or be the means of improving his affairs. If they are in the thick, the consulter may expect to fish in troubled water. Surrounded with dots, his destiny warns him to use diligence, temperance and frugality.

The Lion, or Any Ferocious Beast At the top, in the clear, it signifies prosperity in your intercourse with people of quality. At the bottom, it warns the consulter to shun such intercourse and do nothing to excite any person to envy his fortune.

Worms At the top, or in the middle of the cup, they denote good luck in trade and in matrimony; below, they warn you against rivals in courtship and against enviers in your trade and profession.

The Style If combined with an hour-glass and in the thick, it denotes imminent dangers of all kinds; in love, disappointment; but in the clear, it signifies that your sweetheart is faithful and affectionate towards you, and that you are likely to live a long and happy life.

CHAPTER 4

Fortune Telling by Cards

Many people have striven to fathom Divination, or the art of revealing the secrets of the past, present and future by the aid of cards; but it is to the gypsies one must go if the truth is to be found.

In the following pages I give the authentic method of reading the cards as handed down to the Zingari and used in every gypsy encampment.

Usually only eight cards are used, the Ace ranking highest in value, followed by the King, Queen, Knave, Ten, Nine, Eight and Seven.

The individual meaning attached to the cards follows:

CLUBS

Ace Joy, money, or good news; if reversed, the joy will be of brief duration.

King A frank, liberal man, fond of serving his friends; if reversed, he will meet with a disappointment.

Queen An affectionate woman, but quick-witted and touchy; if reversed, jealous and malicious.

Knave A clever and enterprising young man; reversed, a harmless flirt and flatterer.

Ten Fortune, success, or grandeur; reversed, want of success in some small matter.

Nine Unexpected gain, or a legacy; reversed, some trifling present.

Eight A dark person's affections, which, if returned, will be the cause of great prosperity; reversed, the affections of an undesirable person, and attendant unhappiness, if reciprocated.

Seven A small sum of money, or unexpectedly recovered debt; reversed, a yet smaller amount.

HEARTS

Ace A love letter, or some pleasant news; reversed, a friend's visit.

King A fair, liberal man; reversed, will meet with disappointment.

Queen A mild, amiable woman; reversed, indicates she has been crossed in love.

Knave A gay young bachelor, who dreams only of pleasure; reversed, a discontented military man.

Ten Happiness, triumph; if reversed, some slight anxiety.

Nine Joy, satisfaction, success; reversed, a passing chagrin.

Eight A fair person's affections; reversed, indifference on his or her part.

Seven Pleasant thoughts, tranquility; reversed, tedium, weariness, languor of spirits.

DIAMONDS

Ace A letter soon to be received; reversed, containing bad news.
King A fair man–generally in the army–but both cunning and dangerous; if reversed, a threatened danger, caused by machinations on his part.
Queen An ill-bred, scandal-loving woman; if reversed, she is to be greatly feared.
Knave A tale-bearing servant, or unfaithful friend; if reversed, will be the cause of mischief.
Ten Journey, or change of residence; if reversed, it will not prove fortunate.
Nine Annoyance, or delay; if reversed, either a family or love quarrel.
Eight Lovemaking; if reversed, unsuccessful.
Seven Satire, mockery; reversed, a foolish scandal.

N.B. In order to know whether the Ace, Ten, Nine, Eight and Seven are reversed, make a small pencil mark on each, to show which is the top of the card.

SPADES

Ace Pleasure; reversed, grief, bad news.
King The envious man, an enemy, or a dishonest lawyer, who is to be feared; reversed, impotent malice.
Queen A widow; reversed, a dangerous and malicious woman.
Knave A dark, ill-bred young man; reversed, he is plotting some mischief.
Ten Tears, a prison; reversed, brief affliction
Nine Tidings of a death; if reversed, it will be some near relative.
Eight Approaching illness; reversed, a marriage broken off, or offer refused.

Seven Slight annoyances; reversed, a foolish intrigue.

The Court cards of Hearts and Diamonds usually represent persons of fair complexion; Clubs and Spades, persons of dark complexion.

CARDS OF THE SAME DENOMINATION

Four Aces coming together, or following each other, announce danger, failure in business, and sometimes imprisonment. If one or more of them be reversed the danger is less,

Three Aces coming in the same manner.—Good tidings; if reversed, folly.

Two Aces A plot; if reversed, unsuccessful.

Four Kings Rewards, dignities, honors; revered, they will be less, but sooner received.

Three Kings A consultation on important business, the result of which will be highly satisfactory; if reversed, success will be doubtful.

Two Kings A partnership in business; if reversed, a dissolution of the same. Sometimes this only denotes friendly projects.

Four Queens Company, society; one or more reversed, denotes that the entertainment will not go off well.

Three Queens Friendly calls; reversed, chattering, scandal and deceit.

Two Queens A meeting between friends; reversed, poverty, troubles, in which one will involve the other.

Four Knaves A noisy party—mostly young people; reversed, a drinking bout.

Three Knaves False friends; reversed, a quarrel with some low person.

Two Knaves Evil intentions; reversed, danger.

Four Tens Great success in projected enterprises; reversed, the success will not be so brilliant, but still it will be sure.

Three Tens Improper conduct; reversed, failure.

Two Tens Change of trade or profession; reversed, denotes that the prospect is only a distant one.
Four Nines A great surprise; reversed, a public dinner.
Three Nines Joy, fortune, health; reversed, wealth lost by imprudence.
Two Nines A little gain; reversed, trifling losses at cards.
Four Eights A short journey; reversed, the return of friend or relative.
Three Eights Thoughts of marriage; reversed, folly, flirtation.
Two Eights A brief love-dream; reversed, small pleasures and trifling pains.
Four Sevens Intrigues among servants or low people, threats, snares, and disputes; reversed, that their malice will be impotent to harm, and that the punishment will fall on themselves.
Three Sevens Sickness, premature old age; reversed, slight and brief indisposition.
Two Sevens Levity; reversed, regret.

Any picture card between two others of equal value–as two Tens, two Aces, etc.,–denotes that the person represented by that card runs the risk of prison.

It requires no great effort to commit these significations to memory; but it must be remembered that they are but what the alphabet is to the printed book; a little attention and practice, however, will soon enable the learner to assemble these cards together, and read the events, past and to come, their pictured faces pretend to reveal. The several ways of doing this are here given:

First Method
Dealing the Cards by Threes

Take the pack of thirty-two selected cards (viz., the Ace, King, Queen, Knave, Ten, Nine, Eight and Seven of each suit), having before fixed upon the one you intend to represent yourself, supposing always you are making the essay on your own behalf. If not, it must represent the person for whom you are acting. In doing this, it is necessary to remember that the card chosen should be according to the complexion of the chooser, King or Queen of Diamonds for a very fair person, ditto of Hearts; for one rather darker, Clubs for one darker still, and Spades only for one very dark indeed. The card chosen also loses its signification, and simply becomes the representative of a dark or fair man, woman, as the case may be.

This point having been settled, shuffle the cards, and either cut them or have them cut for you (according to whether you are acting for yourself or another person), taking care to use the left hand. That done, turn them up by threes, and every time you find in these triplets two of the same suit, such as two Hearts, two Clubs, etc., withdraw the highest card and place it on the table before you. If the triplet should chance to be all of the same suit, the highest card is still to be the only one withdrawn; but should it consist of three of the same value but different suits, such as three Kings, etc., they are to be all appropriated. We will suppose that, after having turned up the cards three by three, you have been able to withdraw six, leaving twenty-six, which you shuffle and cut, and again turn up by threes, acting precisely as you did before, until you have obtained either thirteen, fifteen, or seventeen cards. Recollect that the number must always be uneven, and that the card representing the person for whom the essay is made must make one of it. Even if the requisite thirteen, fifteen or seventeen have been obtained, and this one has not made its appearance, the operation must be recommended. Let us suppose the person whose fortune is being read to be a lady, represented by the Queen of Hearts, and that fifteen cards have been obtained and laid out–in the form of a half circle–in the order they were drawn, viz., the Seven of Clubs, the Ten of Diamonds, the Seven of Hearts, the Knave of Clubs, the King of Diamonds, the Nine of Diamonds, the Ten of Hearts, the Queen of Spades, the Eight of Hearts, the Knave of Diamonds, the Nine of Diamonds, the Queen of Hearts, the Nine of Clubs, the Seven of Spades, the Ace of Clubs, the Eight of Spades. Having considered your cards, you will find among them two Queens, two Knaves, two Tens, three Sevens, two Eights, and two Nines; you are, therefore, able to announce:

"The two Queens before me signify the reunion of friends; the two Knaves, that there is mischief being made between them. These two Tens denote a change of profession, which, from one of them being between two Sevens, I see will not be effected without some difficulty; the cause of which, according to these three Sevens, will be illness. However, these two Nines promise some small gain, resulting–so say these two Eights–from a love affair."

You now begin to count seven cards, from right to left, beginning with the Queen of Hearts, who represents the lady you are acting for. The seventh being the King of Diamonds, you may say:

"You often think of a fair man in uniform."

The next seventh card (counting the King of Diamonds as one) proves to be the Ace of Clubs; you add:

"You will receive from him some very joyful tidings; he, besides, intends making you a present."

Count the Ace of Clubs as "one," and proceeding to the next seventh card, the Queen of Spades, you resume:

"A widow is endeavoring to injure you, on this very account; and" (the seventh card, counting the Queen as one, being the Ten of Diamonds) "the annoyance she gives you will oblige you to either take a journey or change your residence; but" (this Ten of Diamonds being imprisoned between two sevens) "your journey or removal will meet with some obstacle."

On proceeding to count as before, calling the Ten of Diamonds one, you will find the seventh card proves to be the Queen of Hearts herself, the person for whom you are acting, and may therefore safely conclude by saying:

"But this you will overcome of yourself, without needing any one's aid or assistance."

Now take the two cards at either extremity of the half circle, which are, respectively, the Eight of Spades and the Seven of Clubs, unite them, and continue:

"A sickness, which will lead to your receiving a small sum of money."

Repeat the same maneuver, which brings together the Ace of Clubs and Ten of Diamonds:

"Good news, which will make you decide on taking a journey, destined to prove a very happy one, and which will occasion you to received a sum of money."

The next cards united, being the Seven of Spades and the Seven of Hearts, you say:

"Tranquility and peace of mind, followed by slight anxiety, quickly succeeded by love and happiness."

Then come the Nine of Clubs and the Knave of Clubs, foretelling: "You will certainly receive money through the exertions of a clever dark young man–Queen of Hearts and King of Diamonds–which comes from the fair man in uniform; this recounter announces some great happiness in store for you, and complete fulfillment of your wishes. Knave of Diamonds and Nine of Diamonds–Although this happy result will be delayed for a time, through some fair young man, not famed for his delicacy–Eight of Hearts and Ten of Hearts–love, joy and triumph. The Queen of Spades, who remains alone, is the widow who is endeavoring to injure you, and who finds herself abandoned by all her friends!"

Now gather up the cards you have been using, shuffle and cut them with the left hand, and proceed to make them into three packs. We will suppose this to be the middle one, and that the cards comprising it are the Knave of Diamonds, the King of Diamonds, the Seven of Spades, the Queen of Spades, and the Seven of Clubs. These, by recollecting our previous instructions regarding the individual and relative signification of the cards, are easily interpreted, as follows:

"The Knave of Clubs–a fair young man, possessed of no delicacy of feeling, who seeks to injure–the King of Diamonds–a fair man in uniform–Seven of Spades–and will succeed in causing him some annoyance–the Queen of Spades–at the instigation of a spiteful woman–Seven of Clubs–but, by means of a small sum of money, matters will be finally easily arranged."

Next take up the left-hand pack, which is "for the house"– the former one having been for the lady herself. Supposing it to consist of the Queen of Hearts, the Knave of Clubs, the Eight of Hearts, the Nine of Diamonds, and the Ace of Clubs, they would read thus:

"Queen of Hearts–the lady whose fortune is being told is, or soon will be, in a house–Knave of Clubs–where she will meet with a dark young man, who–Eight of Hearts–will entreat her assistance to forward his interests with a fair girl– Nine of Diamonds–he having met with delays and disappointments–Ace of Clubs–but a letter will arrive announcing the possession of money, which will remove all difficulties."

The third pack is "for those who did not expect it," and will be composed of four cards, let us say the Ten of Hearts, Nine of Clubs, Eight of Spades, and Ten of Diamonds, signifying:

"The Ten of Hearts–An unexpected piece of good fortune and great happiness–Nine of Clubs–caused by an unlooked-for legacy–Eight of Spades–which joy my perhaps be followed by a slight sickness–Ten of Diamonds–the result of a fatiguing journey."

There now remains on the table only the card intended for the "surprise." This, however, must be left untouched, the other cards gathered up, shuffled, cut, and again laid out in three packs, not forgetting at the first deal to add a card to the "surprise." After the different packs have been duly examined and explained, as before described, they must again be gathered up, shuffled, etc., indeed, the whole operation repeated, after which the three cards forming "the surprise" are examined; and supposing them to be the Seven of Hearts, the Knave of Clubs, and the Queen of Spades, are to be thus interpreted:

"Seven of Hearts–Pleasant thoughts and friendly intentions–Knave of Clubs–of a dark young man–relative to a malicious dark woman, or widow, who will cause him much unhappiness."

Second Method
Dealing the Cards by Sevens

After having shuffled the pack of thirty-two selected cards–which, as we before stated, consist of the Ace, King, Queen, Knave, Ten, Nine, Eight, and Seven of each suit–either cut them yourself, or, if facing for another person, let that person cut them, taking care to use the left hand. Then count seven cards, beginning with the one lying on the top of the pack. The first six are useless, so put them aside, and retain only the seventh, which is to be placed face uppermost on the table before you. Repeat this three times more, then shuffle and cut the cards you have thrown on one side, together with those remaining in your hand, and tell them out in sevens as before, until you have thus obtained twelve cards. It is, however, indispensable that the one representing the person whose fortune is being told should be among the number; therefore, the whole operation must be recommended in case of it not having made its appearance. Your twelve cards being now spread out before you in the order in which they have come to hand, you may begin to explain them as described in the manner of dealing the cards in threes–always bearing in mind both their individual and relative signification. Thus, you first count the cards by sevens, beginning with the one representing the person for whom you are acting, going from right to left. Then take the two cards at either extremity of the line or half-circle, and unite them, and afterward form the three heaps of packs and "the surprise" precisely as we have before described. Indeed, the only difference between the two methods is the manner in which the cards are obtained.

Third Method
Dealing the Cards by Sixteens

After having well shuffled and cut the cards, as we have before said, had them cut, deal them out in two packs, containing sixteen cards in each. Desire the person consulting you to choose one of them; lay aside the first card, to form "the surprise"; turn up the other fifteen, and arrange them in a half-circle before you, going from left to right, placing them in the order in which they come to hand, and taking care to remark whether the one representing the person for whom you are acting be among them. If not, the cards must be all gathered up, shuffled, cut, and dealt as before, and this must be repeated until the missing card makes its appearance in the pack chosen by the person it represents. Now proceed to explain them–first, by interpreting the meaning of any pairs, triplets, or quartettes among them; then by counting them in sevens, going from right to left, and beginning with the card representing the person consulting you; and lastly, by taking the cards at either extremity of the line and pairing them. This being done, gather up the fifteen cards, shuffle, cut, and deal them so as to form three packs of each five cards. From each of these three packs withdraw the topmost card, and place them on the one laid aside to form "the surprise," thus forming four packs of four cards each.

Desire the person for whom you are acting to choose one of these packs, "for herself" or "himself," as the case may be. Turn it up, and spread out the four cards it contains, from left to right, explaining their individual and relative signification. Next proceed in like manner with the pack on your left hand which will be "for the house"; then the third one, "for those who do not expect it"; and lastly, "the surprise."

In order to render our meaning perfectly clear, we will give another example. Let us suppose that the pack for the person consulting you is composed of the Knave of Hearts, the Ace of Diamonds, the Queen of Clubs, and the Eight of Spades reversed. By the aid of the list of meanings we have given, it will be easy to interpret them as follows:

"The Knave of Hearts, is a gay young bachelor–the Ace of Diamonds–who has written, or will very soon write, a letter–the Queen of Clubs–to a dark woman–Eight of Spades reversed–to make proposals to her, which will not be accepted."

On looking back to the list of significations, it will be found to run thus:

Knave of Hearts–A gay young bachelor, who thinks only of pleasure.

Ace of Diamonds–A letter, soon to be received.

Queen of Clubs–An affectionate woman, but quick-tempered and touchy.

Eight of Spades–If reversed, a marriage broken off, or offer refused.

It will thus be seen that each card forms, as it were, a phrase, from an assemblage of which nothing but a little practice is required to form complete sentences. Of this we will give a further example, by interpreting the signification of the three other packs–"for the house," "for those who do not expect it," and "the surprise." The first of these, "for the house," we will suppose to consist of the Queen of Hearts, the Knave of Spades reversed, the Ace of Clubs, and the Nine of Diamonds, which reads thus:

"The Queen of Hearts is a fair woman, mild and amiable in disposition, who–Knave of Spades reversed–will be deceived by a dark, ill-bred young man–the Ace of Clubs–but she will receive some good news, which will console her–Nine of Diamonds–although it is probable that the new may be delayed."

The pack "for those who do not expect it," consisting of the Queen of Diamonds, the King of Spades, the Ace of Hearts reversed, and the Seven of Spades, would signify:

"The Queen of Diamonds is a mischief-making woman–the King of Spades–who is in league with a dishonest lawyer–Ace of Hearts reversed–they will hold a consultation together–Seven of Spades–but the harm they will do soon be repaired."

Lastly comes "the surprise," formed by, we will suppose, the Knave of Diamonds–about to undertake a journey–

Queen of Spades—for the purpose of visiting a widow—Nine of Spades—but one or both of their lives will be endangered.

Fourth Method
The Twenty-One Cards

After having shuffled the thirty-two cards, and cut, or had them cut, with the left hand, withdraw from the pack the first eleven, and lay them on one side. The remainder—twenty-one in all—are to be again shuffled and cut. That done, lay the topmost card on one side to form "the surprise," and arrange the remaining twenty before you, in the order in which they come to hand. Then look whether the card representing the person consulting you be among them; if not, one must be withdrawn from the eleven useless ones, and placed at the right extremity of the row; where it represents the missing card, no matter what it may really be. We will, however, suppose that the person wishing to make the essay is an officer in the army, and consequently represented by the King of Diamonds, and that the twenty cards arranged before you are, the Queen of Diamonds, the King of Clubs, the Ten of Hearts, the Ace of Spades, the Queen of Hearts reversed, the Seven of Spades, the Knave of Diamonds, the Ten of Clubs, the King of Spades, the Eight of Diamonds, the King of Hearts, the Nine of Clubs, the Knave of Spades reversed, the Seven of Hearts, the Ten of Spades, the King of Diamonds, the Ace of Diamonds, the Seven of Clubs, the Nine of Hearts, the Ace of Clubs. You now proceed to examine the cards as they lay, and perceiving that all the four Kings are there, you can predict that great rewards await the person consulting you, and that he will gain great dignity and honor. The two Queens, one of them reversed, announce the reunion of two sorrowful friends; the three Aces, foretell good news; the two Knaves, one of them reversed, danger; the three Tens, improper conduct.

You now begin to explain the cards, commencing with the first on the left hand, viz., the Queen of Diamonds. "The Queen of Diamonds, is a mischief-making, underbred woman–the King of Clubs–endeavoring to win the affections of a worthy and estimable man–Ten of Hearts–over whose scruples she will triumph–Ace of Spades–the affair will make some noise–Queen of Hearts reversed–and greatly distress a charming, fair woman who loves him–Seven of Spades–but her grief will not be of long duration. Knave of Diamonds–An unfaithful servant–Ten of Clubs–will make away with a considerable sum of money–King of Spades–and will be brought to trial–Eight of Diamonds–but saved from punishment through a woman's agency. King of Hearts–a fair man of liberal disposition–Nine of Clubs–will receive a large sum of money–Knave of Spades reversed–which will expose him to the malice of a dark youth of coarse manners. Seven of Hearts–pleasant thoughts, followed by–Ten of Spades–great chagrin–King of Diamonds–await a man in uniform, who is the person consulting me–Ace of Diamonds–but a letter he will speedily receive–Seven of Clubs–containing a small sum of money–Nine of Hearts–will restore his good spirits–Ace of Clubs–which will be further augmented by some good news." Now turn up "the surprise"–which we will suppose to prove the Ace of Hearts–"a card that predicts great happiness, caused by a love letter, but which, making up the four Aces, show that this sudden joy will be followed by great misfortunes.

Now gather up the cards, shuffle, cut, and form into three packs (dealing one card to the surprise), and proceed as before. Repeat the whole operation once more; then take up the three cards forming the surprise, and you then give their interpretation.

We may remark that, no matter how the cards are dealt, whether by threes, sevens, fifteens, or twenty-one, when those lower than the Knave predominate, it foretells success; if Clubs are the most numerous, they predict gain, considerable fortune, etc.; if picture-cards, dignity and honor; Hearts, gladness, good news, Spades, death or sickness. These significations are necessarily very vague, and must, of course, be governed by the position of the cards.

The Italian Method

Take a pack composed of thirty-two selected cards, viz., the Ace, King, Queen, Knave, Ten, Nine, Eight and Seven of each suit. Shuffle them well, and either cut or have them cut for you, according to whether you are acting for yourself or another person. Turn up the cards by threes, and when the triplet is composed of cards of the same suit, lay it aside; when of three different suits, pass it by without withdrawing any of the three; but when composed of two of one suit and one of another, withdraw the highest card of the two. When you have come to the end of the pack, gather up all the cards except those you have withdrawn; shuffle, cut, and again turn up by threes. Repeat this operation until you have obtained fifteen cards, which must be spread out before you, from left to right, in the order in which they come to hand.

Care must, however, be taken that the card representing the person making the essay is among them; if not, the whole operation must be recommenced until the desired result is obtained. We will suppose it to be some dark lady–represented by the Queen of Clubs–who is anxious to make the attempt for herself, and that the cards are laid out in the following order, from left to right: Ten of Diamonds, Queen of Clubs, Eight of Hearts, Ace of Diamonds, Ten of Hearts, Seven of Clubs, King of Spades, Nine of Hearts, Knave of Spades, Ace of Clubs, Seven of Spades, Ten of Spades, Seven of Diamonds, Ace of Spades, Knave of Hearts.

On examining them, you will find there are three Aces among them, announcing good news; but as they are some distance from each other, that the tidings may be some time before they arrive.

The three tens denote that the conduct of the person consulting the cards has not always been strictly correct. The two Knaves are enemies, and the three Sevens predict an illness, caused by them.

You now begin to count five cards, beginning with the Queen of Clubs, who represents the person consulting you. The fifth card, being the Seven of Clubs, announces that the lady will soon receive a small sum of money. The next fifth card proving to be the Ace of Clubs, signifies that this money will be accompanied by some very joyful tidings. Next comes the Ace of Spades, promising complete success to any projects undertaken by the person consulting the cards; then the Eight of Hearts, followed at the proper interval by the King of Spades, showing that the good news will excite the malice of a dishonest lawyer; but the Seven of Spades coming next, announces that the annoyance he can cause will be of short duration, and that a gay, fair young man–the Knave of Hearts–will soon console her for what she has suffered. The Ace of Diamonds tells that she will soon receive a letter from this fair young man–the Nine of Hearts–announcing a great success–Ten of Spades–but this will be followed by some slight chagrin–Ten of Diamonds–to turn her into ridicule. The Queen of Clubs, being representative of herself, shows that it is toward her that the dark young man's malice will be directed. Now take the cards at either extremity of the line, and pain them together. The two first being the Knave of Hearts and the Ten of Diamonds, you may say: "A gay young bachelor is preparing to take a journey—Ace of Spades and Queen of Clubs—which will bring him to the presence of the lady consulting the cards, and cause her great joy. Seven of Diamonds and Eight of Hearts—Scandal talked about a fair young girl. Ten of Spades and Ace of Diamonds—tears shed upon receipt of a letter. Seven of Spades and Ten of Hearts—great joy, mingled with slight sorrow. Seven of Clubs and Ace of Clubs—A letter promising money. Knave of Spades and King of Spades—the winning of a lawsuit. The Nine of Hearts, being the one card left, promises complete success."

Now gather up the cards, shuffle, cut, and deal them out in five packs—one for the lady herself, one for "the house," one for "those who do not expect it," one for "those who do expect it," and one for "the surprise," in the first deal, laying one card aside for "consultation." The rest are then equally distributed among the other five packs, which will four of them contain three cards, while the last only consists of two.

We will suppose the first packet for the lady herself to be composed of the Ace of Diamonds, the Seven of Clubs, and the Ten of Hearts—and containing some very joyful tidings."

The second pack, "for the house," containing the King of Spades, the Nine of Hearts, and the Knave of Spades:

"The person consulting the cards will receive a visit—King of Spades—from a lawyer—Nine of Hearts—which will greatly delight—Knave of Spades—a dark, ill-disposed young man."

The third pack, "for those who do not expect it," composed of the Ace of Spades, the Knave of Hearts, and the Ace of Clubs, would read:

"Ace of Spades–pleasure in store for–Knave of Hearts–a gay young bachelor–Ace of Clubs–by means of money; but as the Knave of Hearts is placed between two Aces; it is evident that he runs a great risk of being imprisoned; and from the two cards signifying respectively 'pleasure' and 'money,' that it will be for having run a debt."

The fourth pack, "for those who do expect it," containing the Eight of Hearts, the Queen of Clubs, and the Ten of Diamonds:

"The Eight of Hearts–the love affairs of a young girl will oblige–the Queen of Clubs–the person consulting the cards–Ten of Diamonds–to take a journey."

The fifth pack, "for the surprise," consists of the Seven of Spades and the Ten of Spades, meaning:

"Seven of Spades–slight trouble–Ten of Spades–caused by some person's imprisonment–The Card of Consolation–Seven of Diamonds–which will turn out to have been a mere report."

Past, Present, Future

The person wishing to try her fortune in this manner (we will suppose her to be a young, fair person, represented by the Eight of Hearts), must well shuffle, and cut with the left hand, the pack of thirty-two cards; after which she must lay aside the topmost and undermost cards, to form the surprise. There will now remain thirty cards, which must be dealt in three parcels–one to the left, one in the middle, and one to the right.

The left-hand pack represents the Past; the middle, the Present, and the one on the right hand, the Future. She must commence with the "Past," which we will suppose to contain these ten cards: The King of Clubs, the Ace of Spades, the Knave of Diamonds, the Nine of Diamonds, the Ace of

Hearts, the Knave of Hearts, the Queen of Hearts, the King of Spades, the Knave of Clubs, and the King of Hearts.

She would remark that picture cards predominating was a favorable sign; also that the presence of three Kings proved that powerful persons were interesting themselves in her affairs. The three Knaves, however, warn her to beware of false friends, and the Nine of Diamonds predicts some great annoyance, overcome by some good and amiable person, represented by the Queen of Hearts. The two Aces also give notice of a plot. Taking the cards in the order they lay, the explanation would run thus:

"The King of Clubs–a frank, open-hearted man–Ace of Spades–fond of gayety and pleasure, is disliked by–Knave of Diamonds–an unfaithful friend–Nine of Diamonds–who seeks to injure him. The Ace of Hearts–a love letter–Knave of Hearts–from a gay young bachelor to a fair, amiable woman–Queen of Hearts–causes–King of Spades–a lawyer to endeavor to injure a clever–Knave of Clubs–enterprising young man, who is saved form him by–the King of Hearts–a good and powerful man. Nevertheless, as the Knave of Clubs is placed between two similar cards, he has run great risk of being imprisoned through the machinations of his enemy."

The second parcel, "the Present," containing the Ten of Diamonds, the Nine of Spades, the Eight of Spades, the Queen of Diamonds, the Queen of Clubs, the Eight of Hearts, the Seven of Spades, the Ten of Spades, Queen of Spades, the Eight of Diamonds, signifies:

"The Ten of Diamonds–a voyage or journey, at that moment taking place–Nine of Spades–caused by the death or dangerous illness of some one–Eight of Spades–whose state will occasion great grief–Queen of Diamonds–to a fair woman. The Queen of Clubs–an affectionate woman seeks to console–Eight of Hearts–a fair young girl, who is the person is the making the essay–Seven of Spades–who has secret griefs–Ten of Spades–causing her many tears–Queen of Spades–these are occasioned by the conduct of either a dark woman or a widow, who–Eight of Diamonds–is her rival."

The third packet of cards, "the Future," we will suppose to contain the Eight of Clubs, the Ten of Clubs, the Seven of Diamonds, the Ten of Hearts, the Seven of clubs, the Nine of Hearts, the Ace of Diamonds, the Knave of Spades, the Seven of Hearts, the Nine of Clubs, which would read thus:

"In the first place, the large number of small cards foretells success in enterprises, although the presence of sevens predicts an illness. The Eight of Clubs–a dark young girl–Ten of Clubs–is about to inherit a large fortune–Seven of Diamonds–but her satirical disposition will destroy–Ten of Hearts–all her happiness. Seven of Clubs–a little money and–Nine of Hearts–much joy–Ace of Hearts–will be announced to the person making the essay by a letter, and–Knave of Spades–a wild young man–Seven of Hearts–will be overjoyed at receiving–Nine of Clubs–some unexpected tidings. The cards of surprise–viz., the King of Diamonds and the Ace of Clubs–predict that a letter will be received from some military man, and that it will contain money.

The Star Method

We will suppose the person making the essay to be a widow, and consequently represented by the Queen of Spades. This card is, therefore, to be withdrawn from the pack and laid, face uppermost, upon the table. The remaining thirty-one cards are then to be well shuffled, cut, the topmost card withdrawn and placed lengthwise, and face uppermost, above the head of the Queen of Spades. The cards are to be shuffled, cut, and the topmost card withdrawn, twelve more times, the manner of their arrangement being this: The Queen of Spades in the center, the first card lengthwise above her head, the second ditto at her feet, third on her right side, the fourth on her left, the fifth placed upright above the first, the sixth ditto below the second, the seventh at the right of the third, the eighth at the left of the fourth, the ninth, tenth, eleventh and twelfth at the four corners, and the thirteenth across the center card–the Queen of Spades–thus forming a star. We will suppose these fourteen cards to be the Queen of Spades, which represents the person making the essay; then–1, the Ace of Hearts; 2, the King of Clubs; 3, the Ten of Clubs; 4, Nine of Diamonds; 5, Queen of Clubs; 6, the Eight of Hearts; 7, the Ten of Spades; 8, the Knave of Clubs; 9, the Seven of Clubs; 10, the Ten of Hearts; 11, the Knave of Diamonds; 12, the Eight of Diamonds; 13, the Nine of Clubs. These being placed at right angles, the person consulting them takes them up two by two, beginning with those last laid down.

The first card, 12, the Eighth of Diamonds, and the one in the opposite corner, viz., 11, the Knave of Diamonds, read: "Overtures will be made–Knave of Diamonds–by a fair young man–next two cards, 10 and 9, Ten of Hearts–which will prove unsuccessful–Seven of Clubs–on account of something connected with money. Next two cards, 8 and 7, the Knave of Clubs–a clever, dark young man–Ten of Spades–will be greatly grieved by 6–Eight of Hearts, a fair girl to whom he is attached. Next two cards, 5 and 4, the Queen of Clubs: A dark woman–Nine of Diamonds–will be annoyed at not receiving, 3–Ten of Clubs–a sum of money–next two cards, 2 and 1, the King of Clubs–which was to have been sent her a generous, dark man, who is fond of obliging his friends been sent her a generous, dark man, who is fond of obliging his friends–Ace of Hearts–it will at last arrive, accompanied by a love-letter–thirteenth card, placed across the Queen of Spades, Nine of Clubs–and be the cause of unexpected gain to the person consulting the cards." There is a shorter and simpler way of doing this, by surrounding the card representing the person trying his or her fortune, with a less number of cards.

The cards are shuffled and cut as before described, and the topmost one withdrawn. We will suppose the center card to be the Knave of Clubs, representing a dark young man–the first topmost one proves to be the Ace of Clubs, and this is placed above the head of the Knave–the second, the Eight of Hearts, is placed at his feet–the third, the Knave of Diamonds, at his right side–the fourth, the Queen of Spades, on his left. These read: "Ace of Clubs–You will soon receive a letter, which will give you great pleasure–Eight of Hearts–from a fair girl. Knave of Diamonds–An unfaithful friend–Queen of Spades–and a malicious widow, will seek to injure you, on that very account."

The English Method

In England the entire pack of cards is used in fortune-telling. The significations also differ in many cases, and I have added a list showing the meanings of the cards when using the whole pack.

CLUBS

Ace Wealth, happiness, and peace of mind.
King A dark man, upright, faithful, and affectionate in disposition.
Queen A dark woman, gentle and pleasing.
Knave A sincere, but hasty friend; also a dark man's thoughts.

Ten Unexpected riches, and loss of a dear friend.
Nine Disobedience to friends' wishes.
Eight A covetous man–also warns against speculations.
Seven Promises good fortune and happiness; but bids a person beware of the opposite sex.
Six Predicts a lucrative business.
Five A prudent marriage.
Four Cautions against inconstancy or change of object for the sake of money.
Three Shows that a person will be more than once married.
Two A disappointment.

DIAMONDS

Ace A letter–from whom, and about what, is seen by the neighboring cards.
King A fair man, hot-tempered, obstinate, and revengeful.
Queen A fair woman, fond of company, and a coquette.
Knave A near relation, who considers only his own interests. Also a fair person's thoughts.
Ten Money.
Nine Shows that a person is fond of roving.
Seven Satire, evil-speaking.
Six Early marriage and widowhood.
Five Unexpected news.
Four Trouble arising from unfaithful friends. Also a betrayed secret.
Three Quarrels, lawsuits, and domestic disagreements.
Two An engagement, against the wishes of friends.

HEARTS

Ace The house. If attended by Spades, it foretells quarreling–if by Hearts, affection and friendship–by Diamonds, money and distant friends–and Clubs, feasting and merry-making.
King A fair man of good-natured disposition, but hasty and rash.

Queen A fair woman, faithful, prudent, and affectionate.
Knave The dearest friend of the consulting party. Also a fair person's thoughts.
Ten Is prophetic of happiness and many children–is corrective of the bad tidings of cards next to it, and confirms good ones.
Nine Wealth and high esteem. Also the wish card.
Eight Pleasure, company.
Seven A fickle and false friend, against whom be on your guard.
Six A generous but credulous person.
Five Troubles caused by unfounded jealousy.
Four A person not easily won.
Three Sorrow caused by a person's own imprudence.
Two Great success; but equal care and attention needed to secure it.

SPADES

Ace Great misfortune; spite.
King A dark, ambitious man.
Queen A malicious, dark woman–generally a widow.
Knave An indolent, envious person; a dark man's thoughts.
Ten Grief, imprisonment.
Nine A card of very bad import, foretelling sickness and misfortune.
Eight Warns a person to be cautious in his undertakings.
Seven Loss of a friend, attended with much trouble.
Six Wealth, through industry.
Five Shows that a bad temper requires correcting.
Four Sickness.
Three A journey.
Two A removal.

REVEALING THE FUTURE

You select the four Kings from a pack, and lay them side by side in a row upon the table.

The lady who wishes to know her fortune gives to each of the cards the name of some gentleman of her acquaintance who might be likely to woo her in marriage. It is usual to pronounce these names aloud before the company. The name given to the King of Hearts is, however, an exception. This secret the lady keeps to herself. To these four Kings, you can also add a Queen, which then denotes the old maid.

Now, take the rest of the pack, shuffle in thoroughly, let the person in question cut three times and commerce. Under each of the above-named picture-cards you lay a card in turn, and as often as a spade is placed under a spade, a heart under a heart, *et cetera*, that is, as often as a card of the same suit is placed under one of these picture-cards, the picture-card is turned from its position.

The first time it takes a direction from left to right, the second time it lies upside down, the third time it is raised again to a position from right to left, and the fourth and last time it regains its former upright position.

That one of the four Kings, who, after these different changes, first resumes his upright position, is to be the happy husband. If it should happen to be the old maid, you can imagine what is in store for you.

After having learned from the cards who is to be the husband, the questions next asked are, usually: How much will he love his wife, why he marries her, and what is his profession. These questions are answered in the following manner:

Gather up the cards, shuffle them thoroughly, and let the person cut them three times. Then tell off the cards upon the table, as you recite the following sentence:

> Heartily, painfully,
> Beyond all measure.
> By fits and starts.
> Not a bit in the world.

You repeat this sentence until the King of Hearts makes his appearance. If it happens that, as you lay this upon the table, you pronounce the word "heartily" he will love his future wife heartily, and so on.

Now as to why he marries her. Count off the cards upon the table, while you repeat the following sentence:

> For love, for her beauty.
> For his parents' command,
> For the bright, golden dollars,
> For counsel of friends.

The sentence by which you discover what is his profession is the following:

> Gentleman, alderman, clergyman, doctor,
> Merchant, broker, professor, major,
> Mechanic, lawyer, ship mast, tailor.

This method of telling fortunes is very entertaining in society, when you have not the book to find more particular answers.

After having shuffled, cut the cards three times, and lay them out in rows of nine cards each. Select any king or queen you please to represent yourself; and wherever you find that card placed, count nine cards every way, reckoning it as one; and every ninth card will prove the prophetic one. Before, however, beginning to count, study well the disposition of the cards, according to their individual and relative signification. If a married woman consult the cards, she must makes her husband the king of the same suit of which she is queen; but if a single woman, she may make any favorite male friend king of whatever suit she pleases. As the knaves of the various suits represent the thoughts of the persons represented by the picture-cards of a corresponding color, they should also be counted from.

WISHES

If it is desired to know whether you will get what you wish for, shuffle the cards, always keeping your thoughts fixed upon whatever wish you may have formed; cut them once, and remark what card you cut; shuffle them again, and deal out into three parcels. Examine each of these in turn, and if you find the card you turned up next either the one representing yourself–the Ace of Hearts or the Nine of Hearts–you will get your wish. If it be in the same parcel with any of these, without being next them, there is a chance of your wish coming to pass at some more distant period; but if the Nine of Spades makes its appearance, you may count on being disappointed.

THE LOTTERY OF LOVE

This interesting and amusing lottery is played with cards and small stakes. Let each one present deposit any trifling sum agreed on; put a complete pack of fifty-two cards, well shuffled, in a bag or reticule. Let the party stand in a circle, and, the bag being handed around, each draw three cards. Pairs of any are favorable omens of some good fortune about to occur to the party, and gets back from the pool the sum that each agreed to pay. The King of Hearts is here made the god of love, and claims double, and gives a faithful swain to the fair one who has the good fortune to draw him; if Venus, the Queen of Hearts, is with him, it is the conquering prize, and clears the pool; five and nines are reckoned crosses and misfortune, and pay a forfeit of the sum agreed on to the pool; besides the usual stipend at each new game; three nines at one draw shows the lady will be an old maid; three fives, a bad husband.

CHAPTER 5

Fortune Telling by Dice

By drawing a horoscope from the spots on the die the gypsies have, after long years of calculation, been able to frame a kind of chart which indicates something of the hidden meaning of the dice. It is not possible to give here in extended detail the results of the gypsies' labors, but a judicious selection has been made of the questions that may be asked and answered, and these are given in the following pages:

Two dice are placed in a box, shaken and then thrown upon the table, the questioner repeating aloud the question he or she wished answered.

The question must be taken from the tables that follow, the answer being found in its proper place, as indicated by the number of spots on the dice thrown.

EXAMPLE

A lady desires to know what sort of a man her husband will be (No. 12). Repeating her question aloud she throws the dice and the spots are:

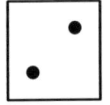 

Look for these corresponding numbers among the answers and you will find that, as No. 12 tells you, the "happy man" will be a little fellow with a heavy beard; made up of conceit and vanity.

QUESTIONS

5. Does the man I love think of me?
6. Will anyone soon pay his addresses to me?
7. What must I do to please him?
8. Shall I answer?
9. Shall I grant what is asked of me?
10. How many admirers shall I have?
11. How many husbands shall I have?
12. What sort of man will my husband be?
13. What does he think of me?
14. May I trust him?
15. Does he love me?
16. Does he think that I love him?
17. Will my heart remain free much longer?
18. Shall I soon receive a letter?
19. Shall I experience many adventures?
20. Shall I be rich?
21. Will my secret be discovered?
22. Am I thought pretty?

THE ZINGARA ART OF DIVINATION

23. Am I thought discreet, witty, interesting?
24. Will he ever become my husband?
25. Shall I do it?
26. Shall I see him soon again?
27. Shall I soon receive a letter?
28. Which of the two shall I choose?
29. Shall I soon receive a present?
30. Shall I soon take a journey?
31. Will my condition shortly be changed?
32. Will my wish be fulfilled?
33. What is he doing at present?
34. What will my husband be?
35. Will it prove a bless to me?
36. Shall I soon receive the wished for tidings?

TABLE OF ANSWERS

5. He thinks much of you as you think of him.

6. Tomorrow morning, about eleven o'clock.

7. Whatever you do, do it gracefully, and especially always treat him with great respect.

8. Yes, but word the reply discreetly.

9. Oh, no, you must not.

10. A dozen at least, sweet little angel. Who would not adore you?

11. One.

12. Young, slender, and fair complexioned.

13. That you are a dear little creature.

14. No, you may not, for he is not good at heart.

15. He cannot help himself.

16. You have let him see it plainly enough.

17. You know very well that it has not been free this long while.

18. In a week.

19. Your life will be peaceful as a quiet lake.

20. You will always have all you need.

21. It would be a good thing if it were discovered.

22. All except your nose, which is too short.

23. Discreet, indeed, but not witty, and interesting only at times.

24. Oh, no!

25. Why not?

26. Tomorrow.

27. Not as soon as you would wish.

28. The one who has the longest nose.

29. Very soon, and it will be a kiss.

30. Yes, a very long one.

31. Yes, to your joy and happiness.

32. It will.

33. He is busy at his toilette, and at this very moment is curling his hair.

34. A rich young gentleman.

35. Yes, it will lead to the purest happiness.

36. Sooner than you expect.

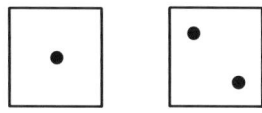

5. He does not in the least.

6. Unfortunately for you, much too soon.

7. Wear always a high-necked dress. Never appear with a bare neck, still less with bare arms–that he hates.

8. It is hazardous.

9. Yes, without the slightest fear.

10. As many admirers as you will have husbands.

11. Two–one squints.

12. Fat and round as a ball. He is exceedingly fond of sweet things, and is of a patient disposition.

13. That your glance has pierced his heart.

14. Have you not had proofs enough that he has the best heart in the world?

15. He is yours, heart and soul.

16. Oh, no, he does not!

17. When you walk out tomorrow, note the first young gentleman you meet who bows to you–he is one with whom you will soon fall in love.

18. In two years

19. Your life will dash onward like a foaming torrent.

20. As rich as you are at present.

21. No, but it were advisable that you disclose it as soon as possible.

22. When you are pleasant and friendly; but when under the influence of temper, you look unattractive.

23. Neither very discreet nor very witty, but to one

person, at least, very interesting.

24. If you will have him.

25. As you please, it will do no harm.

26. Before the autumn wind blows again over the meadow.

27. Yes, but not the one wished for.

28. He who most resembles a porcupine.

29. Yes, a bouquet.

30. You will soon behold cities which you never expected to visit.

31. When you shall wish it changed.

32. If it is really your wish.

33. He is examining his moustache to see how much it has grown during the night.

34. An engineer.

35. No, that is impossible.

36. Not so very soon.

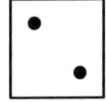 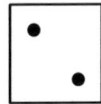

5. Always. In sleep and in dreams, your dear image hovers about him. Even at the breakfast table he beholds your lovely countenance reflected from his buttered bread, and he eats it up for love.

6. Heaven help us! Are you not always surrounded with admirers?

7. Treat him always with frankness and candor, but never act coquettishly.

8. It were better not.

9. You might, but do it prudently.

10. Five–a lame man, a blind man, a deaf man, a dumb man, and a hunchback.

11. One, and a horribly jealous one, who will watch you night and day.

12. Loving and tender; thirty kisses he will daily claim from you.

13. That, in fact, you are really hard-hearted.

14. At all events, you need not mistrust him so very much.

15. Does not his pale countenance betray his deep sorrow?

16. He hopes so, yet he often has doubts.

17. Tomorrow afternoon, around five o'clock. Love's arrow will pierce your bosom.

18. In six weeks.

19. Many thrilling adventures.

20. Quite wealthy.

21. It will, unless you are every moment upon your guard.

22. Very pretty.

23. You are thought to be a good creature.

24. Yes.

25. If it will give you pleasure.

26. No, you are separated forever.

27. There is one now on the way.

28. The one who always gazes upon you with so shrewd an expression.

29. Yes, but it will come from a very different person from the one you think.

30. A short, sentimental one.

31. Yes, but you will be no better off for it.

32. If you do everything in our power to promote it.

33. He is standing before the mirror, and thinks—"After all, my face is well enough, and my figure not bad."

34. A clergyman.

35. It will bring you both joy and sorrow.

36. Never.

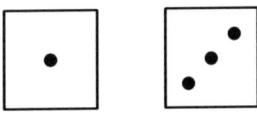

5. Are not your eyes a pair of stars, which he who has once beheld can never forget?

6. Yes, my dear young lady; but be prudent, it is a sad rogue who will next pay attention to you.

7. Show a little more kindness toward human beings, and a little less toward cats.

8. Do so frankly and without affectation.

9. It would be too cruel to refuse.

10. One only, but one who will admire you more than all the rest of mankind together.

11. One, a fat little mushroom of a fellow.

12. Very homely, but in your eyes handsomer than all the world besides—he has lost or will lose half a finger.

13. That it would be dangerous to trust you.

14. Oh, yes, with your whole heart!

15. Do you not see how his cheek reddens when he glances at you?

16. Without a doubt.

17. At the next ball, while dancing a cotillion, your heart will be touched.

18. Never.

19. Too many by far, especially love adventures.

20. You will possess so much wealth, that you will not know what to do with it.

21. It is discovered already.

22. Not beautiful, but very ladylike.

23. You are thought to be a mischievous little vixen.

24. Yes, he and several others.

26. Very soon.

27. The one you would like to receive, you will never receive.

28. The one with the heavy beard.

29. Very soon, a dear, sweet one!

30. Yes, and the one that you are looking forward to with such pleasure.

31. It will depend entirely upon yourself.

32. It will be, certainly.

33. He is drinking a glass of wine to the health of his dear one.

34. A lawyer.

35. It will bring you joy and happiness.

36. Perhaps not in a year yet.

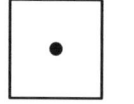

5. He would like to, but he dare not.

6. When you cease your coquetry.

7. The next time you meet him give him your hand and say: "How amiable you are, sir, how handsome! indeed, I am exceedingly happy to be permitted to call you my friend."

8. It would never do to be silent, at any rate; give him a good reprimand.

9. You can not well do otherwise.

10. Two collegians, a tutor, and a captain in the army; perhaps also a fat old merchant.

11. One, and he will be the joy of your life.

12. Very tall, of a light brown complexion, wears spectacles and is the essence of all that is noble, many and amiable.

13. That he can neither comprehend your behavior nor understand your words.

14. You may believe what he says, and not the world's tittle-tattle.

15. That you can find out when you next give him a glass of water; if, in taking it, he tries to touch your hand, he loves you.

16. He thinks so, and is very flattered by it.

17. At this moment your heart is not free–examine it.

18. In a year.

19. Very many, especially with rogues and robbers.

20. Rich in love, rich in all amiable and noble virtues, but not in money.

21. You think that it is a secret, but it never has been one.

22. You pass for it.

23. You are thought to be very capricious.

24. It is hardy possible.

25. It will be of no use, neither will it do you any harm.

26. If you write to him to come and see you, otherwise not.
27. Very soon, and oh, what a tender one!
28. The one who first reaches out his hand to you.
29. Yes, a living one.
30. A journey? Yes, but not the one your thoughts are now dwelling upon.
31. Not so very soon.
32. Yes, but not as soon as you would like.
33. He is enjoying a refreshing slumber.
34. A physician.
35. So long only as you keep your heart pure and true, and without falsehood.
36. Yes, in a few hours.

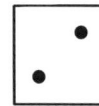 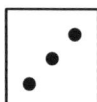

5. Heaven bless me! He has altogether too much to do; he has not time for such thoughts.
6. If you would treat a certain young gentleman with a little more regard, he would take pleasure in so doing.
7. Do not receive so much attention from others.
8. Answer him as such a letter deserves to be answered.
9. Ask your heart, and if it say yes, do you say yes likewise.
10. Your warmest admirers will always be boors.
11. One, a very stout fellow and very unromantic.
12. Very tall and of a dark complexion; somewhat quarrelsome, of a jealous disposition, rather rough, but always having the best intentions.

13. That it would be very dangerous to see you often.

14. Inquire what people say about him. True, there is much falsehood in what is rumored about him, yet something lies at the bottom of it.

15. With his whole heart and soul.

16. Since the last time he saw you he is sure of it.

17. Who knows better than yourself that even now you are in love with him?

18. In five months.

19. Oh, no, very few.

20. You will have money; but, remember, money does not always make on rich, and seldom gives happiness, but is often poison to the heart, and the source of bitter woe.

21. If you tell it to no mortal, no.

22. If you could throw a little more repose into your features while you are speaking, you would be thought so.

23. You are thought to be a genius in every respect, but, for that very reason, you are thought to have many faults.

24. Yes, he will.

25. Oh, by no means! What would people say?

26. At a time when you are the least expecting him.

27. Yes, and it will make you very happy.

28. The one who has the largest hand.

29. Not so very soon.

30. Yes, the journey you are now thinking of.

31. Not in the way to wish.

32. Yes, and sooner than you expect.

33. He is at fisticuffs with his landlord.

34. A scientific man.

35. Certainly, although at first you will not be sensible of it.

36. Within three days, or never.

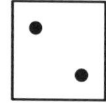 

5. Certainly, quite often, at least, as circumstances permit.

6. You will have wrinkles before that happens to you.

7. Do not put so much sugar in your coffee, or he will think you extravagant.

8. Perhaps you had better, unless you wish to mortify him.

9. Do it, certainly, if you can do it without blushing.

10. Two young students, one dark complexioned, one fair, one of whom will soon present you with a bouquet.

11. Five, and none of them good for anything.

12. A little fellow, with a heavy beard, made up of conceit and vanity.

13. That you would be much more agreeable, if you were not so affected.

14. It is well to be prudent.

15. Oh, yes, but you share his heart with others.

16. Not exactly, but he thinks that he could easily win your heart.

17. For a year yet, but no longer.

18. In six years–not sooner, though you may try ever so hard.

19. Many adventures, but none especially interesting.

20. You will have more than a competence; but, if either you or your husband play at cards for money, you will lose it all.

21. You will betray it yourself.

22. Some few think you homely, some pretty, and one

thinks you beautiful.

23. You are thought to be quick at repartee, but none think you really witty.

24. Yes, if you succeed in winning his heart within two weeks.

25. Do it, but there is one person it will displease.

26. You will have to wait a while.

27. Yes, a very long one.

28. The modest little man.

29. Very soon, and one with which you will be much delighted.

30. Yes, and one that will cost you many tears.

31. Soon, and by an unexpected occurrence.

32. It will be, and more fully than you have reason to expect.

33. He is thinking about some witty speech that he will make when he is next in company.

34. A broker.

35. It will cost you many tears at first, but in the end all will go well.

36. Very soon.

5. He is thinking of you now, and very tenderly.

6. A number, and two or three at the same time.

7. Dress your hair neatly, do not wink so much, sit erect, and be polite to everybody.

8. Place a poppy beneath your pillow tonight, and you will dream what you ought to do.

9. What will a certain person say to it?

10. A dried-up old bachelor whom you cannot endure.//
11. Two—a rickety old fellow, and a wild young man.
12. A man of strong character—energetic and high minded, with wit and humor also.
13. That you have broken his heart.
14. No one deserves confidence better than he does.
15. He is a true friend to you, that is all.
16. He has never thought about it at all.
17. As to your heart, that will be free enough always.
18 Very soon.
19. Many, and many of them interesting ones.
20. If you keep from speculating.
21. If you can, keep it a secret yourself, but you are too much given to blabbing.
22. If you did not wrinkle your nose when you laugh, you would be thought very pretty.
23. You are thought by some peculiar—there is only one person who really understands you.
24. If you can love him truly.
25. Yes, it will cause you much pleasure.
26. Not until you have both gray hairs.
27. Not so very soon, but then it will be a very tender one.
28. The most unpretending one.
29. At present no one thinks of giving you anything.
30. One which will give you much pleasure.
31. Soon, and in a way you never could have dreamed of.
32. Sooner than you expect.
33. He is sighing over the low state of his purse.
34. A farmer.
35. If you are always prudent, thoughtful and cheerful.
36. You know when you have reason to expect it.

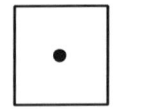 

5. He does; but he will, at some future day, be sorry for it.

6. My dear young lady, congratulate yourself if they do not, for few are worth having.

7. Be not so sentimental, and do not talk so much about poetry and the tender feelings, but show a little practical common sense.

8. What is spoken vanishes, what is written remains.

9. You may grant everything that he asks, for he will ask nothing unworthy of you.

10. Five and twenty–all nice, handsome young gentlemen, five of whom are in love with you already.

11. Three very respectable gentlemen.

12. A horrible fellow–big as a barn door, and in love with himself, because nobody else is.

13. He thinks that you would like to bring him to despair.

14. You would do well to consult your best female friend about it.

15. His heart has long been another's and to her he will never be unfaithful.

16. Oh, no, but he thinks how pleasant it would be if you did love him.

17. Your heart is free at present, but will not be so long.

18. Not until you love a certain person more tenderly than you do at this moment.

19. Yes, and you will in vain sigh for repose.

20. As long as you make good use of your money; if

you cease to do this, your wealth will vanish into air.

21. No, it will not.

22. If you dress your hair plainly, and wear a dark dress, with rose-colored ribbons.

23. Discreet, but very vain and proud.

24. Certainly, if he is not already engaged.

25. Of course, you would be a fool if you did not.

26. Not so very soon.

27. Yes, but the paper has been wet with many tears.

28. The one with the big ears.

29. Some one would like to make you a present, but you will do well not to accept it.

30. An important and joyful occurrence will prevent it.

31. Not very soon.

32. That will depend upon your own conduct–it will, if you act prudently.

33. He is about to hasten to your presence.

34. A letter-carrier.

35. If you do not for an instant lose your presence of mind.

36. No so very quickly.

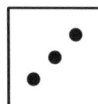 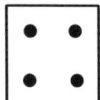

5. Dear creature, he adores you.

6. Yes, but it will not conduce to your happiness.

7. Enjoy your life; be pleasant and gay, like the birds in May.

8. Do so without hesitation.

9. Ask your mother for advise; in such matters she understands what is best.

10. Two–but one has only one eye, and the other has no pose.

11. Only one.

12. Young and handsome, with rosy cheeks; he loves you heartily, and will do anything to please you.

13. He thinks that you have been deceiving him, and cannot conceive for what purpose.

14. Asks some one older than yourself–some female friend.

15. His heart was yours from the first moment that you met.

16. He thinks at least that you would like to have him love you.

17. The next journey you take, you will fall in love.

18. Within two years.

19. Some pleasant ones, and kind friends will protect you from unpleasant ones.

20. No, never.

21. Nobody thinks of inquiring about it.

22. Rather, but without any expression of countenance.

23. You are thought to be the most charming character in the world.

24. He would, if it were not for a certain false friend.

25. Certainly, you can not do better.

26. He is now thinking how to bring about an interview as soon as possible.

27. You will shortly receive a very foolish one.

28. The one with a large mouth.

29. A splendid present, and very shortly.

30. You will have an opportunity to take a journey, but you will not take advantage of it.

31. Yes, and in the way you are now thinking of.

32. It will be your own fault if it is not.

33. He is practicing a speech before the glass.

34. A bookseller.

35. It will be a prelude to the fulfillment of your warmest wishes.

36. You will soon receive it, and shed tears of joy.

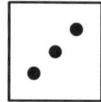

5. He thinks of you, but not in the way you would like to have him.

6. Twenty charming young officers will flock around you within the next two weeks.

7. Walk in the sun without your hat, until you are tanned yellow as an orange.

8. Yes, but give him a good reprimand, for he deserves it.

9. Not wholly, but in part.

10. Fifty, at least, but they are all ugly as sin.

11. Twenty-five, if you take all that offer.

12. Crooked and lame, and as thin as a bean-pole.

13. He thinks: "I will tear your image from my heart, for you do not deserve my love."

14. Heartily and frankly.

15. He loves you, but he resists his passion with all his might, because he does not think he is loved in return.

16. Not that you live him, but that you are a little smitten with him.

17. It will be a long time before you give away your heart, you prude.

18. Within a year.

19. No.

20. Gold will rain down upon you.

21. You had better be upon your guard, for something of it has leaked out already.

22. Lay aside your affection–do not laugh so loud and shrill that you make a person's ears ache, and then you will be quite pretty.

23. You are thought good-natured enough, but vain and silly.

24. If you would flirt less with those young officers, he would gladly be your husband.

25. People will laugh at you, but let not that prevent you.

26. It must be altogether by accident, if at all, for he has sworn never to see you again.

27. You will receive one very soon, but it will be perfectly incomprehensible to you.

28. The one who will soon say to you: "Yes, lady, yes, I swear it!"

29. Yes, one with which you will be much delighted.

30. A sad occurrence will prevent your expected journey.

31. Yes, but not in the way you expect.

32. Wicked people will prevent its fulfillment.

33. He is gaping and thinking to himself: "How dull and tiresome is life."

34. A literary man.

35. It will at first give you much pleasure, but afterward it will cost you a few tears.

36. You will soon receive it, and from one–yes, one– and does not your heart tell you who that one is?

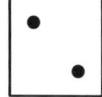 

5. At this moment he is resting his head in his hand, while your image rises to his view.

6. Yes, a bulldog-looking fellow.

7. Pay him a little more attention, and, the next time you meet, take a seat at his right side, and be careful to eat no cheese.

8. Answer what your heart dictates.

9. No, let him pine.

10. Just a dozen, but all old fellows, who have long ago passed the springtime of life.

11. One possibly, but perhaps none.

12. A great favorite at balls and parties, the darling of all the ladies, and yours above all.

13. He thinks: "Why does she always look so coldly upon me? Is it that she cannot endure me?"

14. Has he ever deceived you, that you should distrust him?

15. With pain and longing.

16. He thought so once, but he thinks son no longer.

17. In about six weeks, by starlight, your heart will be softened.

18. In a year or two.

19. A reasonable quantity.

20. Labor always to be rich in discretion and contentedness of mind.

21. It is half discovered already.

22. Stately and beautiful, like a young queen.

23. You are thought original in every respect.

24. No, you need not expect that.

25. If you do not, you are lost.

26. In a few weeks.

27. Yes, in eight days.

28. The one who shortly presents you with a flower.

29. A present which you will soon wish you had never accepted.

30. Soon, and in the company of a young gentleman.

31. In a very agreeable manner.

32. An unexpected accident will prevent its accomplishment.

33. He is fastening his wrist-bands.

34. A man of business.

35. If you are strong enough to repress all pride and vanity on its account, it will prove one.

36. Not so soon as you wish, and other unpleasant tidings will come with it.

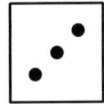 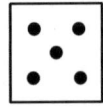

5. More than you think of him.

6. No one worth the having, only a sentimental drover.

7. You must not eat so heartily.

8. There can be no danger in it, at any rate.

9. You would rejoice one heart, and break two—would you do that?

10. Two, a handsome clerk, and a still handsomer young lawyer.

11. One, and you will find him one too many.

12. An old drunkard, and a gambler.

13. He thinks: "She has caused me so much suffering

THE ZINGARA ART OF DIVINATION

that I can never forgive her."

14. Trust him, but still keep your eyes open.

15. He loves you as much as he can, but he cannot love you very much.

16. No, but he thinks you wish him well, as a sister does a brother.

17. Is your heart your own now?

18. In three years.

19. Mischievous persons will prepare many for you.

20. You will have gold pieces by the bushed.

21. If you act discreetly, it will not.

22. You roll your eyes about too much, and your ears are ill-shaped, but your hand is beautiful, and your feet are like a fairy's.

23. You are thought a little foolish, yet prudent enough, and at times somewhat witty and interesting.

24. You do not wish him to be, and he does not wish to be.

25. If you are prudent, it can do no harm.

26. Next fall.

27. Not the one you wish–that will be delayed a little.

28. The noble-looking one, who is so polite and courteous in his manner.

29. A present, over which you will shed tears of joy.

30. Very soon, and in pleasant company.

31. Yes, and exactly to your wishes.

32. It will, and to your infinite happiness.

33. He is daubing his hair with pomatum.

34. A mechanic–probably a shipbuilder.

35. All that happens to us happens as a blessing, but we often misinterpret it.

36. Do not be impatient–They will not come so very quickly.

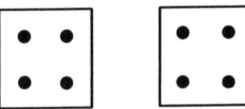

5. You cannot expect that of him, for he never thinks.

6. The first person who meets you tomorrow morning will, from that hour, be your admirer.

7. Fall out with him a little, but never let it be in earnest.

8. If you have discretion enough, answer.

9. Tell your brother the whole affair, and hear what he says. Brothers judge correctly in such cases.

10. One, a stupid little fellow, with yellow hair, and a mouth that stretches from ear to ear.

11. As many as you have had lovers.

12. Handsome and well formed, in the prime of life.

13. That you are a pretty little creature, but much too coquettish.

14. Trust no one blindly in this world.

15. If he could hope to find a return, he would gladly love you.

16. He thinks you are almost dying for love of him.

17. You have been twenty times in love already, and you will be so twenty times more.

18. In three or four years.

19. Storms and calms, as is the way in this world.

20. You will never suffer want, if you are always industrious.

21. No, but by keeping it secret, you will bring upon yourself many disagreeable consequences.

22. Wear a more cheerful countenance, and you would be really beautiful, but an ill-humored expression destroys the prettiest face.

23. Witty and amusing.
24. If he is not your husband, it will be your own fault.
25. Do it, but without much noise.
26. At the next party you are at.
27. If you expect a letter from him, you need not hope for it very soon; he is angry, and it will be long before he forgives you.
28. The one with the pig's eyes.
29. Very soon, and from one you love.
30. Very shortly, and one which will have a decisive influence upon your whole life.
31. If you act prudently in a critical moment which is near at hand, it will.
32. Yes, but to your misfortune.
33. He is writing a love letter.
34. An alderman.
35. If it happens of itself, without your interference, it will be the cause of much happiness to you.
36. It will come some day, but not soon.

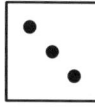 

5. As one thinks of a little, insignificant creature.
6. Yes, a sailor will pay you attention, but this sailor is a rich man's son, who has run away from home to follow the sea.
7. Do what he asks of you the next time you meet.
8. For heaven's sake, no, it will turn out badly for you both.
9. It were better you should not, although it would do no great harm.

10. A rich young planter, and two students.

11. One whom you will have completely under your thumb.

12. A phlegmatic old fellow, who will almost weary the life out of you.

13. That you are pretty and good, and that, if he could love anybody, it would be you.

14. He likes to flirt, but toward you his intentions are honorable.

15. You are his first and his last love.

16. He imagines it possible, at times, because he wishes it so much.

17. For two years yet; do not wish it otherwise.

18. In five years.

19. When you are traveling—not at other times.

20. If you always save up your pennies.

21. There is nothing hid so carefully but it comes to light at last.

22. You are thought to be a masterpiece of heaven's workmanship.

23. Somewhat thoughtless, but good at heart, and of a clear understanding.

24. He will be, and you will live happily together.

25. There is danger in it, certainly, but, if you are very prudent, it may prove fortunate.

26. He will pay you a visit this very day.

27. Not before you have written one.

28. The one who shall first confess or has already confessed his love for you.

29. Yes, and from a person whom you cannot endure.

30. If you wish to, you will have an opportunity.

31. No, not for a long time.

32. Yes, but it will break one person's heart.

33. He is just overturning his inkstand on the table, and he is not a little startled at it.

34. A wealthy country gentleman.

35. Yes.

36. This very day.

 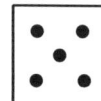

5. You are in his thoughts by day, and in his dreams by night.

6. Not in two years yet.

7. Be gently as a dove, and patient as a lamb–he cannot bear to be opposed and contradicted.

8. That is now a matter of indifference–tears must flow whether you answer or not.

9. If you do, it is much to be feared that, sooner or later, you will greatly regret it.

10. One, a young speculator, tall, slender, and handsome, with black hair and eyes–in short, a paragon.

11. One, a real domestic tyrant.

12. Dry as a herring, and very gluttonous.

13. That you are still quite childish and without discretion.

14. You would mortify him deeply, if you did not.

15. You cannot think to what extent; you should see the tender verses that he daily writes about you.

16. He thinks that all the ladies are in love with him; and you, of course, among the rest.

17. You will fall in love very soon, but it will cost you many tears.

18. In five or six years.

19. Many especially when you attend balls.

20. Not very.

21. Not for a while.

22. That you have a sweet, angelic face–there is nothing more charming to be seen.

23. Possibly so.

24. He would be, if a bitter enemy did not stand between you, and separate you for this world.

25. It will cost you many tears, if you do it, but there will be tears of joy among them.

26. If you visit him–he is displeased, and will not visit you.

27. Your correspondents are all occupied with other matters.

28. The one who will stumble when dancing with you at the next ball.

29. Yes, but a somewhat insignificant one.

30. You will not want for invitations; if you wish it, you will be able to take many journeys.

31. Not in any matter of importance.

32. Yes, but it will make you many enemies.

33. He is railing at his tailor, who will not trust him any longer.

34. A military man.

35. No.

36. Tomorrow, probably, but, if not, next week.

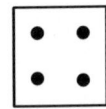 

5. As a person thinks of one with whom he is greatly pleased.

6. Why do you ask? They are all on their knees before you already.

7. Always wear a bouquet of flowers in your bosom, but never in your hair, and, the next time you meet him, place a forget-me-not in his buttonhole.

8. Reflect, my dear young lady, what that might lead to in the end.

9. Do so, with a careless air, and no harm will come of it.

10. In the first place, a little inspector; in the second, a young merchant, the nicest of his kind.

11. One short, one tall, and one of middle stature.

12. Hump-backed, and with a nose as long as your arm.

13. He has always thought you an angel, now he sees that you are his sun, his moon, your eyes are his stars.

16. Yes, but he thinks that you love others besides him.

17. Very soon you will fall in love with a person that you now cannot endure.

18. In seven years.

19. Many, and when you least expect it.

20. For a short time–your own indiscretions will impoverish you.

21. No.

22. When you droop your head, at times, so gracefully, and cast your eyes so prettily to the ground, you are enchanting.

23. No one can venture to dispute that you are the most charming, the most discreet, and the wittiest of mortals.

24. Yes, but you will live rather uncomfortably with him.

25. Alas, it is quite indifferent.

26. He has taken some offense, and for the present will not come.

27. Very soon, a dear, sweet letter.
28. The stoutest.
29. Not for some time.
30. A very, very long one.
31. When the time comes that you wish it.
32. Yes, but it will excite the envy of a certain person, and that will sadden your joy.
33. He is eating buckwheat cakes and sausages.
34. A navel officer.
35. A blessing to you and a delight to your friends.
36. Not the wish for, but very different tidings.

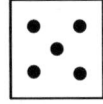 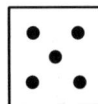

5. Not yet. He will, perhaps, when he has seen you oftener.
6. There is one who is already paying attention to you, but he does it so awkwardly that you do not remark it.
7. If you were to do wonders to please him, he would still see something in you to find fault with.
8. Reflect whether it would be proper.
9. If it will give you pleasure, do so; no one will laugh at you for it.
10. A young merchant, William by name, and two students besides.
11. One, a person whom you already know and love–his name begins with a J.
12. A very funny fellow, full of all sorts of tricks.
13. He thinks: "If I only knew what to do to gain her favor!"
14. Prove him carefully first.

THE ZINGARA ART OF DIVINATION

15. In secret, but he will never venture to let any one perceive it.

16. He thinks so, still he fears your inconstancy.

17. Your heart is not your own at present, but it will soon be free again.

18. This very year.

19. Very soon, a very interesting one.

20. Yes, but if you are not very prudent, you will lose all again.

21. Yes, soon.

22. In the evening, when you are queen of the ball, you are more beautiful than a fairy, for then you strive to shine; but at other times, when you wear your everyday face, you are quite ugly.

23. You are sometimes really silly, but people pardon that in you, for understanding only comes with years.

24. No, he will never marry.

25. Do it, if you take a real pleasure in it.

26. You have too deeply offended him; he will never see you again.

27. In a few days–the most interesting you have ever received.

28. The one who titters the most.

29. Perhaps tomorrow–yet there may be some delay.

30. Just imagine it–a journey to Africa.

31. Somewhat, and agreeably.

32. That will depend upon your behavior.

33. He is sipping a glass of wine, and saying, "How very fine!"

34. A surgeon.

35. It will, at least, cause you many happy hours.

36. If you do not take some pains, never.

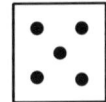 

5. Oh, yes, but with great bitterness.

6. The person who first presents you with a flower will soon pay his addresses to you.

7. Do what you will, it is labor lost, for he is a great fault-finder.

8. At least, wait for another who now asks it of you will be the first to laugh at you.

9. If you do so, the person who now asks it of you will be the first to laugh at you.

10. A young, handsome, slender fellow, called Robert, besides one of your cousins.

11. One, the person whom you now think of the least.

12. A real good-for-nothing, who will give you trouble enough, yet a dear fellow.

13. He thinks: "I do not know what it means, yet she has looked very tenderly at me for some time past."

14. Too much confidence has deceived many a one."

15. Truly and faithfully–you are the sole object of his wishes; to gain your hand, he is laboring in the sweat of his brow.

16. He is much too jealous to be confident of it.

17. Some one will but too soon rob you of your heart and your repose.

18. When the roses bloom again.

19. Not at present, but in course of time.

20. You could become so, if you were resolved upon it.

21. You have nothing to fear.

22. Only in the presence of your lover can you be thought pretty, but then a heavenly angel looks out of your eyes, bathes you in sunshine, and you yourself become an angel.

23. Your heart is pure, your mind clear, and your soul devout.

24. Of course, who else should ever be?

25. Reflect first whether there is not one heart which you would deeply wound by doing it.

26. Very unexpectedly–next month.

27. Early tomorrow morning.

28. The one with a snub nose.

29. Yes, very soon.

30. A delightful journey westward.

31. Not so soon as you expect, nor in the way that you expect.

32. If you wish it very much.

33. He is reading a letter.

34. A carpenter.

35. It is extremely doubtful.

36. Very soon but all your expectations will not be gratified.

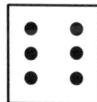 

5. He does not venture, for, when he does, his heart throbs to bursting.

6. Yes, an old gentleman with a wooden leg will soon do so.

7. Let him see that you love him, and prove it to him by sending him a handsome pocketbook.

8. Yes, in a cheerful, jesting style.

9. It would be a step which would have important consequences, yet it will depend upon yourself whether they will be fortunate or unfortunate.

10. In the first place, all your cousins love you, and then a person whom you cannot bear–his name begins with an F.

11. However many you may have, it would be better that you had none.

12. Handsome as an Adonis, and a genius–you are his beau ideal, as he is yours.

13. If she were not so sentimental, she would please me.

14. Whom would you trust, if not him?

15. Just as much as you love him.

16. As often as he sees you, he thinks to himself: "No, she does not love me, she cannot love me.!"

17. Do you not already love as tenderly as one can love?

18. When puss lays an egg.

19. You are so imprudent that it cannot be otherwise.

20. You will always have as much as you have at present.

21. Among your friends there is a Judas who will discover and betray it.

22. You are like a flower, so beautiful, so sweet, so pure!

23. You are thought very artless, the rest time must develop.

24. Do not lose your hold upon him; in the end he must surrender.

25. If you can without blushing.

26. When the spring comes again.

27. In a few weeks, the one longed for.

28. The one who first says: "We met by chance."

29. Some one is thinking about making you one, but it is not certain that anything will come of it.

30. Yes, to Europe.

31. Very soon.

32. Not entirely.

33. He is kissing a little keepsake of yours.

34. An artist or a lieutenant.

35. Decidedly. You will be very happy because of it.

36. The tidings are close at hand, and will be ore agreeable than you can suppose.

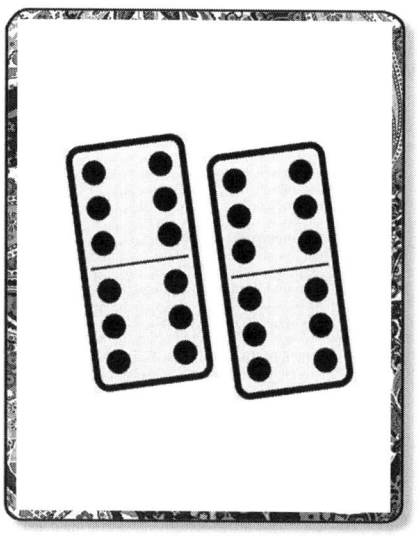

CHAPTER 6

Fortune Telling by Dominoes

The gypsies regard dominoes with a kind of superstitious dread. Few will touch the dotted ivories on Friday or Monday; and a sad fate has befallen those who have consulted this oracle oftener than once a month.

When the dominoes are shuffled, and a card is selected and turned, you will there find written the story of your life. But to repeat the experiment save on the expiration of thirty days is useless, and, as the phrase goes, "unlucky."

Keeping in mind these hints, any one can reveal the future by appealing to the following table of significations.

The dominoes should be well shuffled, to begin with; then let them be spread on the table in the form of a circle, face down. Any domino may then be selected and turned. It is then only necessary to refer to the table for an explanation. Some gypsies insist that the domino farthest away be chosen, but I believe the Fates guide the selection in either case, so that either case, so that either mode will answer the purpose.

WHAT THE DOMINOES INDICATE

DOUBLE-SIX Denotes much riches by speculation, and a happy and prolific marriage. It is not good to farmers as far as relates to crops and success in their calling, but it foretells that their lands will rise in value, and that they can make money by selling out. If a girl turns this domino to learn her fate in matrimonial matters, it is a sign that she will marry rich, and have a large family of children.

SIX-FIVE If you are in search of employment, this domino shows that you will succeed by proper perseverance. If in love, do not be discouraged by an rebuffs, for success awaits you. If you have planted a crop, or are about to plant one, it will yield nobly. In money matters exclusively, you may not be fortunate, as the domino is not lucky for money. If your wife is about to give birth to a child, and you try your fortune with special reference to such birth, this domino foretells its early death. If you are about to buy real estate, you will be lucky in the purchase–if to buy silverware, jewelry, or a watch, you will get cheated. If you expect a legacy, you will probably be lucky and get it.

SIX-FOUR This domino denotes early marriage and much happiness; the sexes of the children will be about equally divided, and they will live, but will leave home early–the girls to marry, and the boys to do for themselves. It denotes neither poverty nor riches.

THE ZINGARA ART OF DIVINATION   91

SIX-THREE This domino denotes constancy and affection. It is an excellent domino for lovers, who will marry early, and enjoy much happiness. It is also a sign of riches and honors; and no troubles of any account will mar your fortune. There is some danger, however, that you will die at middle age, but, if you survive that period, you will live to a good old age.

SIX-TWO Is an excellent domino for lovers, as it foretells a happy marriage. A gentleman turning this domino will get an orderly and economical wife, and a lady will have equal good fortune in a thrifty and industrious husband. Those who turn this domino for luck in business matters will realize all and more than they expect. To dishonest and selfish people, however, the domino is fatal. If it is turned to determine the result of any scheme that is not fair and above-board, it foretells ill-success and exposure. To a married lady who expects to present her husband with an heir, it presents a beautiful and healthy child, and one who will excel as a mathematician, and (if a boy) will probably become distinguished.

SIX-ONE This domino foretells to young people that they will marry twice, and the second marriage will be the happiest of the two. To married people it is a sign that they will be better off in middle age than when young, and that one child will be faithful and remain with them, while their others will seek their fortunes away from home.

SIX-BLANK If you turn this domino you will hear of the death of an esteemed friend, or an acquaintance–will experience the loss of a relative or member of your family–or some one will die in whom you are interested. To a farmer, or the owner of horses or other animals, it may denote the loss of some of the animals rather than human beings; but it foretells death in some shape, and may even mean to warn you of your own decease.

DOUBLE-FIVE Is a decidedly lucky domino in everything you undertake. It foretells success in all enterprises, but does not assure you that you will become rich.

FIVE-FOUR This domino shows to a lady that she will probably marry a poor man, have a large family of children, and then become a widow. He may be pretty well off, to appearance, when she marries him, but if it be so, she will find that he has debts and expensive habits that will bring him to poverty and the grave. It is not a good domino for money matters, for if you have lost money, or if people owe you, the turning of this domino shows that you will not be apt to get the cash. To a farmer it is a sign of good crops; but it is also a sign that something unfortunate will occur in connection with the farm, such as cattle lost or injured, or property of some kind destroyed.

FIVE-THREE Denotes ample means, without any other peculiarity of fortune. If you turn this domino you may calculate you will never be poor, and may become quite wealthy. But to one already wealthy, it shows that though he may not become poor, he will never be any better off then he is, and perhaps not so well off. To young people the domino denotes comfortable circumstances after marriage, but not over-zealous love. It shows no positive bad luck in love matters, at the same time that it does not assure you of devoted attachment of your proposed partner for life, of either sex. On the whole, it is a pretty fair domino for any one to turn.

FIVE-TWO If you are in love, you will probably be unfortunate; for though you may get the person you want, and an apparently happy marriage may follow, it will prove an unhappy one in the end. Nevertheless, your happiness may continue for some time after marriage. To a gentleman this domino foretells a thrifty and industrious wife, though one with an unhappy temper or disposition. To a single lady it denotes thrift and independence as long as she remains single. If a man is engaged in speculation, or is about to start any new enterprise, he will not be likely to succeed. If you are a candidate for office you will be defeated. On the whole, this is not a pretty fair one.

FIVE-ONE It is a jolly domino for persons fond of excitement. It predicts that you will receive an invitation to a dinner, or social gathering, or to some place where you will enjoy yourself. If a married lady turns this domino it is a sign that she will present her husband with a triple addition to his family–all boys. To a young lady it predicts a beau, who will not be rich or refined, but rather a rough customer, and she will discard him and marry another. If you expect to earn or to receive money, this domino is one of disappointment.

FIVE-BLANK If a man turn it, he will be either a gambler or a rich rogue, if he has brains enough, and, if his intellect is not sufficient, he will probably be a small swindler, or the favored lover of a lewd woman, or both. Although these will be his characteristics, yet circumstances may place him in a different position; but he will always be mercenary, selfish, impudent, and without pride of character. To a girl this domino foretells an unhappy marriage, and misfortune by that means; but if she remains single, and keeps clear of lovers, she will avoid the ill omen.

DOUBLE-FOUR It is a good and smooth domino for lovers, for farmers and for laboring people of all kinds. On the contrary, lawyers, doctors or professionals who turn it, will probably have a spell of hard times to encounter. To little girls and boys it predicts that they will soon be invited to a party, and have much pleasure. If any one is about to give a party, and turns this domino, he or she may count on a first-rate time, for everything will go on well, and the party will be a decided success. It likewise predicts that a wedding will come off very soon.

FOUR-THREE Those who turn this domino will marry young, live happily and will not probably have more than one child that will live. To a couple who are childless, it is a sign of a second marriage. If a married person who has children turns this domino, it is a sign that the family will be reduced by death or long absence.

FOUR-TWO Foretells a change in your circumstances, condition, family, relations or your ideas. It is not know what the change will be, but there will really be a change, fate has ordained. It may be nothing at all serious, or it may be something that will affect your whole life. For instance, a young person who turns this domino may get married–that will be an important change, but whether the marriage will be a happy one, is not known. A married person may lose their partner–a man may fail in business, or may become pious and join the church–a family may break up housekeeping and take board, or may lose a favorite child. Indeed, a thousand little incidents may occur in life which will cause a change in your usual routine. To farmers and persons who work hard for a living, the change will probably be a favorable or happy one. To rich and lazy people it will be an unfortunate one. To any other than these two classes it is uncertain what the nature of it will be. If you have offended your lover, or any particular friend, this domino shows that you will soon makeup and become stronger friends than ever. It is a lucky domino for farmers and business matters, although it does not point out any particular good fortune that awaits them.

FOUR-ONE Those who turn this domino will marry happily, and no uncommon event will mar their nuptials; the omen connected with it usually points to childless couples who are well off; and I find that where children are born, the parties will lose their wealth and position in proportion to the number of their offspring, which will never exceed four. In most cases there will be no children, but ample means.

FOUR-BLANK Is an unfortunate domino for lovers, as it foretells quarrels and separations, old maids and old bachelors. A girl who has a lover, and turns this domino to find out his peculiarities, had better look somewhere else at once, for she will certainly either lose or discard him. It is the same with a gentleman–he will never marry a girl he then expects to, and may be jilted. To married people the domino gives a prolific promise. A married lady who turns it will probably have twins or triplets at her next maternity. If you think to entrust a secret to a friend, this domino denotes that it will not be kept. It also foretells that your future husband or wife will be a very credulous person—perhaps a believer in Spiritualism or some other doctrine.

DOUBLE-THREE Denotes immense riches, but has no allusion to matrimony. It is an excellent domino for any one to turn, as it points to money in abundance, and does not intimate any unhappiness; therefore, the person who turns it will get plenty of cash, and be happy or not, as fate may ordain.

THREE-TWO Is a fortunate domino in the following cases: Marriage, love-making, recovering stolen property, going on a journey, entering into a speculation, planting a crop, collecting a debt, or making a purchase. This domino shows also that you may be lucky in collecting some old claim or debt that you had given up as lost. It is bad for gamblers, for a woman about to give birth to a child, and for peddlers.

THREE-ONE A young girl who turns this domino will be in danger of losing her chastity; therefore let her be careful. A married woman turning it will have an outside admirer who will flatter here with a view to an improper intimacy. To a man it foretells the loss of money through his illicit intercourse with the opposite sex. It is not a favorable domino to any one.

THREE-BLANK This domino denotes that your sweetheart is artful and deceitful. If you get married, your wife will be either shrewish, or vain and unprincipled, and perhaps run away and disgrace you. To a girl it foretells a putty-head of a husband—one who is easily influenced, and whom she can wind round her finger. If you turn this domino, it is a sign you will soon be invited to a party and there make a new acquaintance, with whom you will afterward have a quarrel. If a married man or woman turns it, it predicts a family quarrel.

DOUBLE-TWO The turning of this domino denotes success in love matters and much happiness in the married state, together with good children who will live and be prosperous. It also denotes success in any undertaking, and thrift, though not great riches.

TWO-ONE The turning of this domino denotes to a lady that she will marry young, and that her husband will die, leaving her a large property, and childless. For a long time she will be a gay, rich widow, but will be caught at last, and marry happily. To a young man it denotes a life of luxury; he will never marry, but will be a favorite of the ladies, and have several mistresses. It is not a good domino for business men, as it foretells losses by failures.

TWO-BLANK The turning of this domino denotes poverty and bad luck. To a marriageable young woman it predicts a poor, dissipated and dishonest husband. On the birth of a child–if a boy, it is a sign that he will be poor and shiftless, and perhaps dishonest–if a girl, that she will not marry well. It is not a bad domino for a girl who lives unmarried, for she may do very well alone. It is a domino of good luck to thieves and bad people. If they turn it, it is a sign of success in any dishonest undertaking. Should you turn this domino in reference to a journey, it shows that you will go in safety. It predicts an easy deliverance in case you are attacked, and should be obliged to defend yourself.

DOUBLE-ACE Denotes affectionate constancy and happiness in the marriage state. It is an excellent domino to turn, both for lovers and married people, as besides the above it indicates a competency of this world's goods.

DOUBLE-BLANK To turn this domino is the worst sign in the whole set, and is only favorable to misers, useurs, gamblers and unprincipled cheats and seducers. To any heartless, selfish person, the turning of this domino foretells good luck–to all others disappointment. We hope that no young girl turning a domino to ascertain her fortune as to marriage will turn this one, for it surely foretells disappointment and sorrow. If she has a lover, and should he marry her, he will desert her afterward. In business matters, too, it is decidedly unfavorable, and is a sign that your business will decrease. If you are wanting a situation, you will not be likely to get it, and if anything is lost or stolen, it will not probably be recovered again. It is generally a pretty bad domino for decent people, but a good one for all the dishonest ones, who, if they have got anything by trickery and fraud, will be apt to enjoy it.

CHAPTER 7

The Meaning of Dreams

There can hardly be any doubt that the future is often revealed by dreams. There have, of course, been many extravagant fictions palmed off as facts relative to dream, but yet enough credible evidence exists of their importance to make any singular dream the subject of reflection and examination by the dreamer. For example, a man dreams he is at a ball dancing with an unknown lady. A few days later the ball is a reality, and before the year is out, the lady is his wife. Had he consulted a soothsayer about his dream, he would have learned the result long before it had come to pass. Dreams often work contrariwise; a pulpit in a vision means a place of disrepute; a wedding means a funeral, and punishment foretells good fortune. A love-lorn damsel dreams that she is absorbed in a book. If she could fathom the meaning, she would take heart, for such a dream presages a romantic marriage and a life full of joy. Some dreams are meant as warnings. If birds are seen flying around a tower, it means that the dreamer should be prepared for trouble. To dream of having a sword indicated that you will do well to save every cent you can, for the day is near at hand when your income will be cut off.

These are only a few examples to show the grave importance of dreams. The subject is too vast to be touched upon here, but I would advise my readers to procure a few reliable dream books and to continue to research the subject.

CHAPTER 8
Lucky and Unlucky Days

One method of determining the lucky and unlucky days of any month in the year is to first ascertain from the almanac the day on which a full moon occurs, and count the number of days from that to the end of the month; you then multiply the number of days in the month by the number ascertained as above, and the total will give you the lucky days (subject to a further test hereafter explained), which must be reckoned this wise: If the total happens to be, say, 516, the lucky days of that month would be the 5th and 16th, and if it would be 561, the days are the same, for you must always transpose the figures, when they will work together. Suppose that instead of 516, the total should be 399; as neither of these figures can be paired, the lucky days from that total are the 3rd and 9th, and the 9th would be considered doubly lucky, if no tests worked to the contrary.

The unlucky days are determined in precisely the same manner, by multiplying the number of days in the month by the number which had passed previous to a full moon.

After working out your list of lucky days, in the manner above described, you must then test them, in order to be sure that there are not opposing influences. You can do this by calculating the unlucky days. Should you find that any day of the month which was designed as lucky came also in the list of unlucky days, the latter preponderates and you must strike it from the lucky list.

This plan of demonstrating lucky and unlucky days is very ancient, and has been tested to such an extent that it is considered accurate by most astrologers. In old times, before the mass of the people understood much about figures, the professional fortune tellers demanded a large fee for casting the lucky days of any month, which they accomplished in the manner above described.

Lucky marriage days for girls were cast in the same manner, except that the age of the girl was used as the multiplier, instead of the number of days in the month. The result was determined similarly, and also by a test of the unlucky days. Thus, if a girl is 18 years old, and thinks of marrying in October, she takes up an almanac and ascertains the day of the full moon in that month. It occurs on the 24th, and there are 31 days in the month; this leaves 7 for the multiplier. She multiplies this by her age, 18, and the result is 106, which shows the lucky days in that month for her to marry are the 10th and the 6th, unless they are destroyed by the test, which is determined as follows: There are 23 days before the 24th, and she must multiply 23 by 18, which gives 414, and shows

THE ZINGARA ART OF DIVINATION 103

that the 4th and 14th are the only unlucky days for her to marry; and as they do not conflict with the lucky days, the 6th and 10th may be considered as genuine lucky days for that month, reckoning the moon to have fulled on the 24th. In determining her age, she should reckon any period over half a year a full year.

Females born on the following days may expect courtship and prospects of marriage with a happy termination:

January 1, 2, 15, 26, 27, 28.
February 11, 21, 25, 26.
March 10, 24.
April 6, 15, 16, 20, 28.
May 3, 13, 18, 31.
June 10, 11, 15, 22, 25.
July 9, 14, 15, 28.
August 6, 7, 10, 11, 16, 20, 25.
September 4, 8, 9, 17, 18, 23.
October 3, 7, 16, 21, 22.
November 5, 14, 20.
December 14, 15, 19, 20, 22, 23, 25.

LUCKY HOURS

Persons born within the limits of the succeeding list of hours, on any of the preceding days, will be the most likely to marry:

January 2nd. From 30 minutes past 10 till 15 minutes past 1 in the morning; and from 15 minutes before 9 till 15 minutes before 11 at night.

January 15th. From 30 minutes past 9 till 15 minutes past 10 in the morning; and from 30 minutes past 7 till 15 minutes past 11 at night.

January 26th. From 30 minutes past 8 till 15 minutes past 9 in the morning; and from 7 till 15 minutes past 10 at night.

February 11th and 12th. From 30 minutes past 7 till 15 minutes past 8 in the morning; and from 15 minutes past 6 till 15 minutes before 9 at night.

February 21st. From 7 till 15 minutes before 8 in the morning; and from 15 minutes past 5 till 15 minutes before eight at night.

February 25th and 26th. From 15 minutes before 7 till 30 minutes past 7 in the morning; and from 15 minutes before 5 till 30 minutes past 7 in the evening.

March 10th. From 5 till 15 minutes before 6 in the morning; and from 4 in the afternoon till 15 minutes before 7 in the evening.

April 6th. From 15 minutes past 4 till 5 in the morning; and from 30 minutes past 2 till 15 minutes past 5 in the afternoon.

April 20th. From 30 minutes past 3 till 15 minutes past 4 in the morning; and from 30 minutes past 1 till 15 minutes past 4 in the afternoon .

May 3rd. From 15 minutes before 3 till 30 minutes past 3 in the morning; and from 15 minutes before 1 till 30 minutes past 3 in the afternoon.

May 13th. From 2 till 15 minutes before 3 in the morning; and from 12 at noon till 15 minutes before 3 in the afternoon.

May 18th. From 15 minutes before 1 till 30 minutes past 2 in the morning; and from 15 minutes before 12 at noon till 30 minutes past 2 in the afternoon.

May 31st. From 15 minutes before 1 till 30 minutes past 1 in the morning; and from 15 minutes past ten in the morning till 15 minutes before 1 in the afternoon.

June 10th and 11th. From 15 minutes past 10 till 1 in the afternoon; and from 12 at night till 1 in the morning.

June 15th. From 10 in the morning till 2 in the afternoon; and from 15 minutes before 12 at night till 15 minutes before 1 in the morning.

June 25th. From 15 minutes past 9 in the morning till 12 at noon; and from 11 to 12 at night.

June 29th. From 9 in the morning till 15 minutes before 12 at noon; and from 15 minutes before 11 till 15 minutes before 12 at night.

July 9th. From 15 minutes past 8 till 11 in the morning; and from 10 till 11 at night.

July 14th and 15th. From 8 till 11 in the morning; and from 10 till 11 at night.

July 28th. From 7 till 10 in the morning; and from 9 till 10 at night.

August 6th and 7th. From 30 minutes past 6 till 15 minutes past 9 in the morning; and from 15 minutes past 8 till 15 minutes past 9 at night.

August 10th and 11th. From 15 minutes past 6 till 9 in the morning; and from 8 till 9 in the evening.

August 19th and 20th. From 30 minutes past 5 till 30 minutes past 8 in the morning; and from 30 minutes past 7 till 30 minutes past 8 in the evening.

August 25th From 15 minutes past 5 till 8 in the morning; and from 7 till 8 in the evening.

September 4th. From 15 minutes before 5 till 30 minutes past 7 in the morning; and from 30 minutes past 6 till 30 minutes past 7 in the evening.

September 8th and 9th. From 30 minutes past 4 till 15 minutes past 7 in the morning; and from 15 minutes past 6 till 15 minutes past 7 in the evening.

September 17th and 18th. From 5 till 15 minutes after 5 in the morning; and from 15 minutes before 6 till 15 minutes before 7 in the evening.

September 23rd. From 30 minutes past 3 till 30 minutes past 5 in the morning; and from 30 minutes past 5 till 30 minutes past 6 in the evening.

October 3rd. From 3 till 15 minutes before 6 in the morning; and from 15 minutes past 4 till 15 minutes past 5 in the afternoon.

October 7th. From 15 minutes before 3 till 30 minutes past 5 in the morning; and from 30 minutes past 4 till 30 minutes past 5 in the afternoon.

October 16th. From 2 till 5 in the morning; and from 4 till 5 in the afternoon.

October 21st and 22nd. From 15 minutes before 2 till 30 minutes past 4 in the morning; and from 30 minutes past 3 till 15 minutes past 4 in the afternoon.

November 5th. From 1 till 15 minutes before 4 in the morning; and from 15 minutes before 3 till 15 minutes before 4 in the afternoon.

November 14th. From 15 minutes past 12 till 3 in the morning; and from 2 till 3 in the afternoon.

November 20th. From 15 minutes before 12 minutes past 2 in the morning; and from 15 minutes past 1 till 2 in the afternoon.

December 14th and 15th. From 10 till 30 minutes past 12 in the morning; and from 12 at noon till 15 minutes before 1 in the afternoon.

December 18th and 19th. From 15 minutes before 10 at night till 15 minutes past 5 in the morning; and from 30 minutes past 11 till 15 minutes past 12 at night.

January 3rd. From 30 minutes past 10 till 15 minutes past 11 in the morning; and from 15 minutes before 9 till 15 minutes past 11 at night.

January 12th and 13th. From 15 minutes past 9 till 10 in the morning; and from 15 minutes before 8 till 30 minutes past 10 at night.

January 18th. From 9 till 15 minutes before 10 in the morning; and from 15 minutes past 7 till 10 at night.

January 27th. From 9 till 15 minutes before 10 in the morning; and from 7 till 15 minutes before 10 at night.

February 1st. From 8 till 30 minutes past 8 in the morning; and from 6 till 30 minutes past 8 in the evening.

February 11th and 12th. From 15 minutes before 8 till 30 minutes past 8 in the morning; and from 15 minutes before 6 till 30 minutes past 8 in the evening.

February 17th. From 7 till 15 minutes before 8 in the morning; and from 15 minutes past 5 till 8 in the evening.

March 1st. From 30 minutes past 6 till 15 minutes past 7 in the morning; and from 30 minutes past 4 till 15 minutes past 7 in the evening.

March 16th and 17th. From 30 minutes past 5 till 15 minutes past 6 in the morning; and from 15 minutes before 4 till 30 minutes past 6 in the evening.

March 19th, 20th, 21, 22nd, 23rd, 24th and 25th. From 30 minutes past 5 till 30 minutes past 6 in the morning; and from 30 minutes past 3 till 15 minutes past 6 in the evening.

March 26th, 27th, 28th, 29th and 30th. From 15 minutes past 5 till 15 minutes before 6 in the morning; and from 15 minutes past 3 till 6 in the evening.

April 3rd, 4th, 5th, 6th, 7th, 8th and 9th. From 30 minutes past 4 till 30 minutes past 5 in the morning; and from 30 minutes past 2 till 5 in the afternoon.

April 10th, 11th, 12th, 13th, 14th. From 15 minutes before 4 till 15 minutes before 5 in the morning; and from 2 till 30 minutes past 4 in the afternoon.

April 19th, 20th, 21st, 22nd and 23rd. From 30 minutes past 4 till 30 minutes past 5 in the morning; and from 15 minutes before 2 till 30 minutes past 4 in the afternoon.

April 25th, 26th, 27th, and 28th. From 3 till 4 in the morning; and from 15 minutes past 1 till 15 minutes before 4 in the afternoon.

May 3rd, 4th, 5th, 6th, 7th, and 8th. From 15 minutes past 2 till 15 minutes past 3 in the morning; and from 30 minutes past 12 at noon till 15 minutes past 3 in the afternoon.

May 9th, 10th, 11th, 12th, and 13th. From 2 till 3 in the morning; and from 15 minutes past 12 at noon till 3 in the afternoon.

May 16th, 17th, 18th, 19th, 20th, 21st and 22nd. From 15 minutes before 2 till 15 minutes before 3 in the morning; and from 12 at noon till 15 minutes before 3 in the afternoon.

May 23rd, 24th, 25th, 26th, and 27th. From 15 minutes past 1 till 15 minutes past 2 in the morning; and from 30 minutes past 11 in the forenoon till 15 minutes past 2 in the afternoon.

June 1st, 2nd, 3rd, 4th, 5th, and 6th. From 15 minutes past 10 in the morning till 1 in the afternoon; and from 15 minutes past 12 at night till 15 minutes past 1 the next morning.

June 11th. From 15 minutes past 10 in the morning, till 15 minutes before 1 in the afternoon; and from 12 at night till 1 the next morning.

June 20th. From 30 minutes past 9 in the morning till 12 at noon; and from 11 to 12 at night.

June 25th. From 15 minutes past 9 in the morning till 12 at noon; and from 11 to 12 at night.

July 5th. From 15 minutes before 8 till 15 minutes past 10 in the morning; and from 15 minutes before 10 till 15 minutes before 11 at night.

July 6th. From 15 minutes past 8 till 11 in the morning; and from 15 minutes past 10 till 11 at night.

July 19th. From 30 minutes past 7 till 10 in the morning; and from 15 minutes past 9 till 15 minutes past 10 at night.

July 24th. From 7 till 15 minutes before 10 in the morning; and from 9 till 10 at night.

August 2nd and 3rd. From 30 minutes past 6 till 15 minutes before 9 in the morning; and from 30 minutes past 8 till 30 minutes past 9 at night.

August 6th. From 15 minutes before 6 till 9 in the morning; and from 30 minutes past 7 till 30 minutes past 8 at night.

August 22nd. From 15 minutes past 5 till 8 in the morning; and from 15 minutes past 7 till 15 minutes past 8 at night.

September 1st. From 4 till 15 minutes before 7 in the morning; and from 6 till 7 in the evening.

September 5th. From 30 minutes past 4 till 15 minutes before 7 in the morning; and from 30 minutes past 6 till 30 minutes past 7 in the evening.

September 14th. From 15 minutes before 4 till 30 minutes past 6 in the morning; and from 30 minutes past 5 till 30 minutes past 6 in the evening.

September 29th. From 15 minutes before 3 till 30 minutes past 5 in the morning; and from 30 minutes past 4 till 30 minutes past 5 in the evening.

October 3rd. From 3 till 15 minutes before 6 in the morning; and from 15 minutes before 5 till 15 minutes before 6 in the evening.

October 12th. From 15 minutes past 2 till 5 in the morning; and from 15 minutes before 4 till 30 minutes past 4 in the afternoon.

October 18th and 19th. From 30 minutes past 1 till 4 in the morning; and from 15 minutes before 3 till 30 minutes past 4 in the afternoon.

November 10th and 11th. From 30 minutes past 12 at night till 15 minutes past 3 in the morning; and from 30 minutes past 1 till 30 minutes past 2 in the afternoon.

November 15th and 16th. From 12 at night till 15 minutes before 3 in the morning; and from 15 minutes past 1 till 2 in the afternoon.

November 29th and 30th. From 15 minutes pasts 11 at night till 2 in the morning; and from 1 till 15 minutes before 2 in the afternoon.

December 8th and 9th. From 15 minutes past 10 at night till 1 in the morning; and from 30 minutes past 12 at noon till 30 minutes past 1 in the afternoon.

December 14th, 15th and 16th. From 10 at night till 15 minutes before 1 in the morning; and from 30 minutes past 12 at noon till 30 minutes past 1 in the afternoon.

December 23rd and 24th. From 15 minutes past 11 till 12 at noon; and from 15 minutes past 8 till 12 at night.

December 28th. From 15 minutes past 10 till 11 in the morning; and from 9 till 15 minutes before 12 at night.

It has often been recorded, and though a singular observation, experience has shown it to be a true one, that some event of importance is sure to happen to a woman in her thirty-first year, whether single or married; it may prove for her good, or it may be some great evil or temptation; therefore, we advise her to be cautious and circumspect in all her actions. If she is a maiden or widow, it is probable she will marry this year. If a wife, that she will lose her children or husband; she will either receive riches or travel into a foreign land; and at all events, some circumstance or other will take place during this remarkable year of her life that will have great effect on her future fortunes and existence.

The like is applicable to men in their forty-second year, of which so many instances have been proved that there is not a doubt of its truth. Observe always to take a lease for an odd number of years; even are not prosperous. The three first days of the moon are the best for signing papers, and the first five days as well as the twenty-fourth for any fresh undertaking. But we cannot but allow that a great deal depends on our own industry and perseverance, and by strictly discharging our duty to God and man, we may often overcome the malign influence of a bad planet or a day marked as unlucky in the book of fate.

UNLUCKY BIRTHDAYS FOR MALES
January 3 and 4.
February 6, 7, 12, 13, 19 and 20.
March 5, 6, 12 and 13.
May 12, 13, 20, 21, 26 and 27.
June 1, 2, 9, 10, 16, 17, 22, 23 and 24.
July 3, 4, 10, 11, 16, 17 and 18.
October 3, 4, 9, 10, 11, 16, 17 and 31.
November 1 and 3.

Almost all men that are born on the days included in the foregoing table, will, in a greater or less degree suffer, not only by pecuniary embarrassment and losses of property, but will also experience great distress and anxiety of mind, much dissatisfaction, dissension and unhappiness in their family affairs, much disaffection to each other among the married ones (indeed, few of them can ever be happy in the married state), trouble about their children, daughters forming unfortunate attachments, and a variety of untoward events of other descriptions. The influence of these days are of a quality and tendency calculated to excite in the minds of persons born on them an extraordinary itch for speculation, to make changes in their affairs, commence new undertakings of various kinds, but all of them will tend nearly to one point–loss of property and pecuniary embarrassments. Such persons who embark their capital on credit in new concerns or engagements, will be likely to receive checks or interruptions to the progress of their schemes or undertakings. Those who enter into engagements intended to be permanent, whether purchases, leases, partnerships, or, in short, any other speculation of a description which cannot readily be transferred, or got rid of, will dearly repent their bargains.

They will find their affairs from time to time much interrupted and agitated, and experience many disappointments in money matters, trouble through bills and have need of all their activity and address to prop their declining credit; indeed, almost all engagements and affairs that are entered upon by persons born on any of these days will receive some sort of check or obstruction. The greater number of those persons born on these days will be subject to weakness or sprains in the knees and ankles, also diseases and hurts in the legs.

UNLUCKY BIRTHDAYS FOR FEMALES

January 5, 6, 13, 14, 20 and 21.
February 2, 3, 9, 10, 16, 17, 22 and 23.
March 1, 2, 8, 9, 16, 17, 28 and 29.
April 24 and 25.
May 1, 2, 9, 17, 22 and 30.
June 5, 6, 12, 13, 18 and 19.
July 3 and 4.
September 9 and 16.
October 20 and 27.
November 9, 10, 21, 29, and 30
December 6, 14 and 21.

Females born on these days should be extremely cautious of placing their affections too hastily, as they will be subject to disappointments and vexations in that respect; it will be better for them in those matters to be guided by advice of their friends, rather than by their own feelings. They will be less fortunate in placing their affections than in any other action of their lives, as many of these marriages will terminate in separations, divorces, etc. Their courtships will end in elopements, seductions and other ways not necessary of explanation.

The list of days above given will be productive of hasty and clandestine marriages–under untoward circumstances, perplexing attachments, and, as a natural consequence, the displeasure of friends, together with family broils, dissensions and divisions.

CHAPTER 9

The Language of Flowers

It is to the gypsies that the world must come if they would know the hidden meaning in the rose or the daisy.

The following table is that used by the Zingari; it is prepared with great care, and should always be consulted when sending, receiving or dreaming of flowers:

Acacia Blossom. Come to my heart!

Aconite, Blue. Flatterer! are you to be trusted?

Aconite, Yellow. Your caprice is unendurable.

Alpine Rose. Love must venture; timidity can never win.

Amaranth. The earthly only can become the spoil of the grave; love is immortal, and belongs to heaven.

Anemone. My thought by day, and my dream by night.

Anemone Wood. Your cruelty is destroying me.

Anise. You must mend your manners.

Apple Blossom. Who plucks the blossoms, destroys his hopes of fruit.

Apricot Blossom. Are you always so gay, so trifling?

Aster. Weep no longer, you will find him again above the stars.

Aspen Leaf. Your heart beats for every one, therefore no heart beats for you.

Auricula. Who would not love you?

Balsam. Splendor dazzles, grace alone enchains.

Balsam Rose. Let my image dwell always in your heart.

Barley. Come again tomorrow.

Bean Blossom. Forgive me, I misunderstood you.

Birch Branch. How sweetly are sorrow's tears dried up on the bosom of a sympathizing friend.

Blackberry Branch. Contentment and love.

Bluebottle. Be simple and humble, and life will always appear to you in heavenly colors.

Boxwood. I hope continually.

Buckwheat Blossom. Not idle show, quite domestic virtues alone insure lasting happiness.

Burr. Like seeks like.

Buttercup. Your presence is consoling to me.

Cabbage Leaf. When you come again, come sober.

Camomile. Could you, then, love anybody beside yourself?

Carnation. How I burn!

Centaury. You seek money only–I will not waste my love upon you.

Cherry Blossom. When will love tinge your cheeks?

Chestnut Blossom. Always as today.

Clover Blossom. I will live for you.

Columbine. Your words sound well, but what says your heart?

Crown Imperial. Let me be your slave, and I am happy.

Cuckoo Flower. I like not long complainings.

Currant Twig. Whoever loves me must share my sorrow, and respect my grief.

Cypress. When my heart is broken, and I lie in the cold grave, give me at least a tear.

Daffodil. Let me not pine!

Dill. Love strengthens–I will protect you.

Elder Blossom. Your fidelity is destined to a sweet reward.

Fig Leaf. I am ashamed.

Flax. Do you love me for myself?

Foxglove: None but a fool could be as forward as you.

Gillyflower. Where you are, it is always spring.

Grape Vine. Fear not! Love conquers!

Grass. Love for love, truth for truth.

Hazel Twig. Forgive me!

Hearts Ease. Because I feel friendship for you, you imagine that I love you–you are in error.

Heather Blossom. I ask only for your friendship.

Heliotrope. Give me proofs of your love.

Honeysuckle. Eternal fidelity! When shall we meet again?

Hyacinth–Single. When I am dead, you will regret your cruelty.

Hyacinth–Double. Heaven shines in your eyes; the angels listen to your words.

Hydrangea. And you could so soon forget me!

Immortelle. True love is unchangeable.

Iris. Why have you disturbed the peace of my heart?

Ivy. I am ever true.

Jasmine. Can calm, domestic happiness content you?

Larkspur. Your love is my aim.

Laurel. You have my heart.

Lemon Blossom. Give me hope!

Lily–Tiger. My heart burns.

Lily–White. Angel, let me adore you.

Linden Blossom. I am favorably inclined to you.

Maple Twig. What is more painful than to be misunderstood by one you love?

Marigold. I like you not.

Marshmallow. To fondle is not to love.

Mignonette. Not beauty, but goodness of heart is my choice.

Mullen. If you love me, I envy not a king's crown.

Mushrooms. Away! go home, and cry about it!

Myrtle Blossom. Be constant; sweet is the reward of love.

Myrtle Branch. Will you be my wife (husband)?

Nettle. Beware! coquetry has its penalty.

Oak Leaf. My fidelity bids defiance to every storm.

Oats. Return.

Oleander. True until death.

Parsley. You are in love with me.

Peony. You are too vain–and of what?

Pine. In vain you strive to gain my confidence–stern fate has made me rude and silent.

Pink-Carthusian. Why so reserved?

Pink-Variegated. Friendship is all that I can feel for you.

Pomegranate Blossom. A kiss.

Poppy. I cannot endure you–you are too stupid.

Potato Blossom. Modest worth surpasses outward show.

Primrose. Give me your love–I will cherish it faithfully and in secret.

Ranunculus. Where you are, there is my home.

Ribbon Grass. Give me a kiss.

Rocket. Sleep visits not my eyelids; I wake and long for you.

Rose–Monthly. Every month you have a new love.

Rose–Red. You pass like a conqueror through the world.

Rose–White. Beautiful are you in childlike innocence, more beautiful will you be when warmed by the breath of love.

Rosebud. Your presence fills me with heavenly longing.

Rose Petal–Red. Yes!

Rose Petal–White. No!

Rosemary. You were absent–life departed; you returned–I live again.

Snowdrop. You have kindled the first sparks of love in my bosom.

Strawberry. Not earthly rank gives happiness, but worth and amiability.

Sweet Pea. You name is inconstancy.

Sweet William. Light and hasty impressions are soon effaced.

Thistle. Your words offend me; you have deeply wounded me.

Thyme. I have not understood you.

Veronica. What would this world be without you?

Violet. I love you for your gentle modesty.

Wintergreen. Remain constant and true–then we will meet again.

Wood Sorrel. You brighten my existence as the stars brighten the night.

CHAPTER 10

The Meaning of Moles

A person's character can generally be told by the moles that appear on his or her body. The larger the mole the greater the prosperity or adversity indicated. If the mole is round, it signifies good; if oblong, a moderate share of good fortune; if angular, a fair proportion of good or evil; the deeper the color, the more pronounced the favor or disgrace. If the mole is very hairy, much misfortune is in store; if only a few hairs grow upon it, undertakings will be successful.

Following is a list showing the signification of moles:

Ankle. Shows an effeminate disposition, given to foppery in dress and cowardice in a man; but in a woman it denotes courage, wit and activity–they foretell success in life with an agreeable partner, accumulation of honors and riches, and much pleasure in the affairs of love.

Arm. On either arm it reveals a courteous disposition, fortitude, resolution, industry, and conjugal fidelity; it foretells that the person will fight many battles, and be successful in all; that you will be prosperous in your undertakings, obtain a decent competency, and live very happy–it denotes that a man will be a widower at forty, but in a woman it shows that she will be survived by her husband.

Armpits. You will be very good looking, will become rich and be benevolent.

Back. If just below either of the shoulder blades, it signifies that you will have misfortune and defeat in the enterprise you may undertake.

Belly. Shows an indolent, slothful disposition, given to gluttony, very selfish, addicted to the pleasures of love and drink, negligent of dress, and cowardly; it denotes small success in life, many crosses, some imprisonment, and traveling, with losses by sea; but it foretells that you will marry an agreeable partner of a sweet temper, have children, who will be industrious and become very respectable in life.

Bosom. Shows a quarrelsome and unhappy tempter, give to low debauchery, and exceedingly amorous, indolent and unsteady; it denotes a life neither very prosperous nor very miserable, but passed without many friends or much esteem.

Breast. A mole on the right breast shows an intemperate and indolent disposition, rather given to drink, strongly attached to joys of love; it denotes much misfortune in life, with a sudden reverse from riches to poverty–many unpleasant and disagreeable accidents, with a sober and industrious partner–many children, mostly girls, who will all marry well, and be a great comfort to your old age; it warns you to beware of pretended friends, who will harm you much. A mole on the left breast shows an industrious and sober disposition, amorous, and much given to walking; it denotes great success in life and in love, that you will accumulate riches and have many children, mostly boys, who will make their fortunes at sea.

A mole under the left breast, under the heart, shows a rambling, unsettled disposition, given to drinking and little careful of your actions; very amorous, and much given to indulge indiscriminately in the pleasures of love, in a man. In a woman it indicates sincerity in love, industry and a strict regard for character; in life it denotes a varied mixture of good and bad fortune, the former rather prevailing; it denotes imprisonment for debt, but not of long duration. To a woman it denotes easy labors, and children who will become rich, live happy and respected, and marry well.

Buttocks Signifies shiftlessness and poverty, though a good capacity; it is a sign that you will be too lazy to do anything for yourself.

Cheek. A mole on either cheek shows an industrious, benevolent and sober disposition, given to be grave and solemn, little inclined to amorous sports, but of a steady courage and unshaken fortitude; it denotes a moderate success in life, neither becoming rich nor falling into poverty; it also foretells an agreeable and industrious partner, with two children, who will do better than the parents.

Chin. A mole on the chin shows an amiable and tranquil disposition, industrious and much inclined to traveling, and the joys of Venus; it denotes that the person will be highly successful in life, accumulating a large and splendid fortune, with many respectable and worthy friends, and agreeable conjugal partner, and fine children, but also indicates losses by sea and in foreign countries.

Ear. On either ear it denotes riches in man or woman. If on the lower tip of the ear, keep off the water, or you will be drowned.

Elbow. A mole on either elbow shows a restlessness and unsteady disposition, with a great desire for traveling– much discontented in the married state and of an idle turn; it indicated no very great prosperity, rather a sinking than rising condition, with many unpleasant adventures, much to your discredit–marriage to a person who will make you unhappy, and children who will be disobedient, and cause you much trouble.

Eye. A mole on the outside corner of either eye shows a sober, honest and steady disposition, much inclined to the pleasures of love; it foretells a violent death, after a life considerably varied by pleasures and misfortunes; in general it foreshadows that poverty will keep at distance.

Eyebrow. A mole on the right eyebrow signifies a sprightly, active disposition, a great turn for gallantry, much courage, and great perseverance; it denotes wealth and success in love, war and business; that you will marry an agreeable mate, live happy, have children, and die in an advanced old age, at a distance form home. On the left eyebrow, temple, or side of the forehead, shows an indolent, peevish temper, a turn for debauchery and liquor, little inclined to amorous sports, and very cowardly; foretells poverty, imprisonment and disappointments in all your undertakings, with undutiful children and a bad-tempered partner.

Finger. On either finger of either hand, it shows that you will be a thief, or a dishonest person in some way, and never wealthy.

Foot. A mole on either foot shows a melancholy and inactive disposition, little inclined to the pleasures of love, given to reading and a sedentary life; they foretell sickness and unexpected misfortunes, with many sorrows and much trouble, an unhappy choice of a partner for life, with disobedient and unfortunate children.

Forehead. If the mole is in the center of the forehead, it predicts an active, industrious disposition, success in business, riches, honors, a happy marriage, and a son who will be distinguished. But if the mole is on the side of the forehead, the signification is not so favorable, particularly if on the left side. (See Eyebrow.) On the right side of the forehead, or right temple, shows an active and industrious disposition, much given to the sports of love; it denotes that she will be very successful in life, marry an agreeable partner, and arrive at unexpected riches and honors, and have a son, who will become a great man.

Groin. On the right groin denotes riches and honors, but to be accompanied by disease. On the left groin, you will have the sickness without the wealth.

Gullet. On that part of the throat called the gullet, it predicts that you will be distinguished in some way and become rich.

Hand. Moles on either hand, if not on the fingers, denote wealth, industry and energy in either sex. You will also be fortunate and happy in your children.

Heart. Over the heart, denotes wickedness, poverty and a hasty, headstrong disposition. (See Breast).

Heel. Shows a spiteful and malevolent disposition, but a person of much energy, who may be successful in what he undertakes; that he will be greatly talked about behind his back.

Hip. A mole on either hip shows a contented disposition, given to industry, amorous and faithful in engagements, of an abstemious turn; it foretells moderate success in life, with many children, who will undergo many hardships with great fortitude, and arrive at ease and affluence by dint of their industry and ingenuity.

Instep. Shows that you will be quarrelsome and have few friends. Also a great walker.

Knee. A mole on the left knew shows a hasty and passionate disposition, extravagant and inconsiderate turn, with no great inclination to industry and honesty, much given to pleasures of Venus, but possessed of much benevolence; ;it indicates good success in undertakings, particularly in contracts, a rich marriage, and an only child. On the right knee, shows an amiable temper, honest disposition and a turn for amorous pleasures and industry; it foretells great success in love, and the choice of a conjugal partner, which few sorrows, many friends and dutiful children.

Leg. Moles on either leg show a person of a thoughtless, indolent disposition, of an amorous turn, much given to extravagance and dissipation; it denotes many difficulties through life, but that you will surmount them all; it shows that imprisonment will happen to you at an early age, but that in general you will be more fortunate than otherwise;

you will marry an agreeable person, who will survive you, by whom you will have four children, two of whom will die young.

Lips. A mole on either lip shows a delicate appetite, a sober disposition, and much given to the pleasures of love, of an industrious and benevolent turn; it denotes that the person will be successful in undertakings, particularly in love affairs–that you will rise above your present condition, and be greatly respected and esteemed–that you will endeavor to obtain some situation, in which you will at first prove unsuccessful, but afterward prevail.

Mons. If a woman has a mole here, she will become the mother of a great genius, or else the wife of a distinguished personage. It is also a sign of riches.

Mouth. (See Lips.)

Navel. On a woman it denotes many children, a good husband, and an abundance of this world's goods. On a man it is a sign he will be lucky in all he undertakes, become very rich, and that he will have a son who will be distinguished.

Neck. In front of the neck is a good sign; you will rise to unexpected honors and dignities, or become rich. On the back of the neck it denotes misfortune. On either side of the neck it foretells that you will become wicked or quarrelsome; and if on the right side, behind the ear, it is a sign that you will be hung.

Nipple. In a woman it is a sign that she will have a child that will become famous and distinguished in the world. In man it denotes that he will be fond of women, and spend much of his life in amours, to the neglect of his proper business.

Nose. Moles on any part of the nose show a hasty and passionate disposition, much given to amorous pleasures, faithful to engagements, open, and sincere in friendship, courageous and honest, but very petulant, and rather given to drink; it denotes great success through life and in love affairs–that you will become rich, marry well, have fine children and be much esteemed by your neighbors and acquaintances–that you will travel much, particularly by water.

Nostril. Inside the nostril shows that you will be energetic and persevering, and well off in the world; that you will get a good wife or husband when you marry.

Private Members. Moles on these parts show a generous, open and honest disposition, extremely disposed to gallantry and the joys of Venus given to sobriety, and of undaunted courage; it denotes great success in the latter part of life, but many and severe misfortunes in the former, which will be borne with fortitude; it also foretells a happy marriage and fine children, who will be happy, thrive well, and grow rich and respectable; in man it shows that he will have natural children, who will cut a great figure in life, but he will experience much plague and vexation from their mother.

Shin. (See Leg.)

Shoulder. On the left shoulder shows a person of a quarrelsome, unruly disposition, always inclined to dispute for trifles, rather indolent, but much inclined to the pleasures of love, and faithful to the conjugal vows. It denotes a life not much varied either with pleasures or misfortunes; they indicate many children, and moderate success in business, but dangers by sea. On the right shoulder shows a person of a prudent and discreet temper, one possessed of much wisdom, given to great secrecy, very industrious, but not very amorous, yet faithful to conjugal ties; it indicates great prosperity and advancement in life, a good partner, and many friends, with great profit from a journey to a distant country, about the age of thirty-five.

Side. On either side, near any part of the ribs, shows an indolent, cowardly disposition, given to excessive drinking, of an inferior capacity, and little inclined to the pleasures of love; it denotes an easy life, rather of poverty than riches, little respected, a partner of an uneven and disagreeable temper, with undutiful children, who will fall into many difficulties.

Stomach. If in the pit of the stomach, it shows a person of foppish disposition, with little common sense, though much industry; it also denotes riches. If lower down on the stomach, it is a sign that you will promise more than you will perform, but will, nevertheless, be highly esteemed.

Thigh. On the right thigh, it shows the person to be of an agreeable temper, inclined to amorous, and very courageous; it also denotes success in life, accumulation of riches by marriage, and many fine children, chiefly girls. On the left thigh, shows a good and benevolent disposition, a great turn for industry, and little inclined to the pleasures of love; it likewise indicates many sorrows in life, great poverty, unfaithful friends, and imprisonment by the false swearing of some one.

Throat It predicts a fortunate and wealthy marriage to either sex. (See Neck.)

Tongue. If a man shall have a mole on his tongue, it foretells that he shall marry with a rich and beautiful woman of great celebrity. On a woman's tongue it denotes reserve of manner and wisdom; also a fortunate marriage.

Wrist. Moles on the wrist, or between that and the finger ends, show the person to be of an ingenious and industrious turn, faithful in his engagements, amorous and constant in his affections, rather of a saving disposition, with a great degree of sobriety and regularly in his dealings. It foreshows a comfortable acquisition of fortune, with a good partner, and beautiful children, but some disagreeable circumstances will happen about the age of thirty, which continue four or five years. In a man, it denotes being twice married–in a woman, only once, but that she will survive her husband.

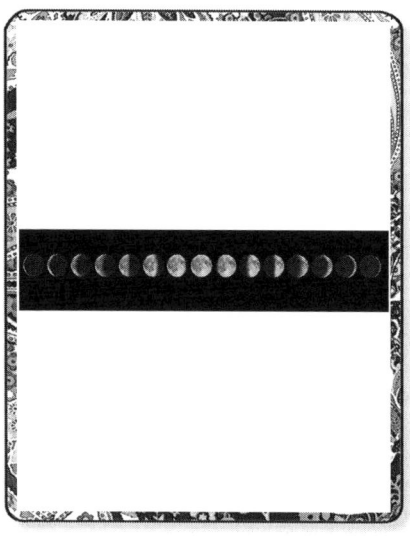

CHAPTER 11

The Moon's Age

1. A child born within twenty-one hours after the new moon will be fortunate and live to a good old age; whatever is dreamt on this day will be fortunate and pleasant to the dreamer; various undertakings will succeed on this day.

The following numbers, for example, 2, corresponds to the second day after the new moon and so forth and not the second day of the month.

2. This is a very lucky day for discovering things lost or hidden; the child born on this day will thrive, but the dreams are not to be depended upon.

3. A child born on this day will be fortunate through persons in power, and all dreams will prove true.

4. This day is bad; persons failing on this day rarely recover; the dreams will have no effect.

5. This day is favorable to begin a good work, and the dreams will be tolerably successful; the child born on this day will be vain and deceitful.

6. The dreams of this day will not immediately come to pass; and the child born will not live long.

7. Do not tell your dreams on this day; if sickness befall you on this day you will soon recover; the child born will live long, but have many troubles.

8. Dreams of this day will come to pass; business begun on this day will prosper, and anything lost will be found.

9. This day differs from the former, the child born on this day will acquire great riches and honor.

10. This day is likely to be fatal; those who fall sick will rarely recover; the child born on this day will be devoted to religion, and of an engaging form and manner; if a female, she will possess an uncommon share of wisdom and learning; this day is good to begin a journey, to marry, or to engage in business.

11. Dreams on this day are fortunate; and the child born will live long, and be very sensible; but a person who falls sick on this day rarely recovers.

12. Dreams on this day will quickly prove true.

13. If you ask a favor on this day, it will be granted.

14. The sickness that befalls a person on this day is likely to prove mortal; what was lost yesterday may be found today.

15. The child born on this day will be of ill manners and unfortunate; it is a good day for dealing in merchandise.

16. The child born on this day will be foolish; it is an unlucky day to marry, or to begin any kind of business on.

17. The child born on this day will be very valiant, but will suffer hardships; if a female, she will be chaste and industrious, and live respected to a great age.

18. This day is dangerous; the child born will be dishonest.

19. Dreams on this day will be vain and untrue; the child born will grow up healthy and strong, but be of a selfish and ungentle turn of mind.

20. The child born will be fortunate, and of a cheerful countenance, religious, and much beloved; any kind of business begun on this day will be unfortunate.

21. The child born on this day will be of an ungovernable temper, forsake his friends, wander in a foreign land, and be unhappy through life; it is a happy day to marry on; and all business begun on this day will be successful.

22. The child born on this day will be wicked, meet with many dangers, and come to an untimely end; it is a very unfortunate day, and threatens everything with disappointment and crosses; whoever falls sick on this day seldom recovers.

23. Dreams on this day are certain; and the child born on this day will be rich and greatly esteemed.

24. This day is favorable for dreams; and the child born will be of a sweet and amiable disposition.

25. This day is bad for dreams, and those who fall sick on it are in great danger; the child born on this day will be its parents' delight, but will not live to any great age.

26. This day is good for dreams, but children born on it will experience many hardships, though, in the end, they may turn out happily.

27. This is a very unfortunate day to look for anything that is lost, but a child born on this day will make a great stir in the world, either as a statesman, soldier, physician or clergyman.

28. A child born upon this day will live to be a rich and truly good man, if born before noon; but, if born after that hour, it is to be feared that he will be dissipated or worthless.

29. Dreams on this day are not worth a moment's attention, for, rest assured, they will never be fulfilled. Never buy a lottery ticket on this day.

CHAPTER 12

Omens

It would be futile to attempt to collect all the petty circumstances that are regarded as omens, but I give a few of the more important, indicating their source where possible. Lucky and unlucky days are treated of elsewhere in this book. Such so-called omens are the spilling of salt and walking under a ladder are too trivial for comment. Do not, however, be misled by the many small omens that you have laughed at. Read the accompanying list carefully, and you will discover there is more truth in omens than you have supposed.

It is considered an ill omen when one sees a spider in the morning. The earlier in the morning; and the larger the spider, the greater the evil which threatens you. It is within doors, however, and chiefly in one's own chamber, that the spider has this signification—out of doors they forebode no harm. The wood spider especially is not much to be dreaded; what I said above refers particularly to the house spider. Never, on an account, kill a wood spider. By such an act you would only draw upon yourself the hatred of the whole race of witches, and, sooner or later, you would suffer from it.

When found in the evening, a spider signifies good luck. The smaller the spider, the greater good fortune. I will here teach you the following rhyme:

"Matin, chagrin.

Soir, espok."

Little spiders have much less evil in them than the others, and those called daddy-long-legs are always messengers of good luck.

If your shoe-tie or apron-string breaks, your sweetheart is thinking of you.

If your right ear tingles, someone is speaking well of you; if the left ear tingles, someone is speaking ill of you. To find out who this someone is, you must call out aloud the names of your acquaintances, one after another. The name at which the tingling ceases is the name of the person.

If your nose itches early in the morning, you will on that very day hear a piece of news.

Lay under your pillow a prayer-book, opened at the matrimonial service, bound round with the garters you wore that day, and a sprig of myrtle on the page that says "With this ring I thee wed," and your dream will be ominous, and you will have your fortune as well told as if you had paid a dollar to an astrologer.

If any one tells you anything, and you are shortly after

obliged to sneeze, you may be sure that what was told you is true.

If you hear a wood tick or death-watch ticking anywhere in the house, you must try to get rid of it as soon as possible, or you will speedily hear of a death which will greatly afflict you.

"Nail gifts" are white specks on the finger nails, which, according to their respective situations, are believed to predict certain events, as indicated in the following couplet, which is repeated whilst touching the thumb and each finger in success:

"A gift, a friend, a foe.

A lover to come, a journey to go."

Sometimes the augury is expressed in positive terms, as:

"A gift on the thumb is sure to come.

A gift on the finger is sure to linger."

This mode of prognostication is of long standing. Melton, in his "Astrologaster," a very old work, giving a catalogue of many superstitious ceremonies, tells us that "to have yellow speckles on the nails of one's hands is a greate signe of death." In Reed's old plays we read:

"When yellow spots do on your hands appear,

Be certain then you of a corse shall hear."

Sneezing has been held ominous from times of the most remote antiquity.

The comet of 590 was, according to some authors, the occasion of a custom which is extensively diffused among all the nations of Christendom. In the year of this comet a frightful plague prevailed, which was alleged to be due to its influence. While the malady was at its height a sneezing was frequently followed by death; whence they say, "God bless you!" with which, since that time sneezers are saluted. St. Austin tells us that "the ancients were wont to go to bed again if they sneezed while they put on their shoes." Aristotle says: "Sneezing from noon to midnight was good, but from night to noon unlucky."

"Love knots" are spells or charms made of the blades of the oat or wheat, and sometimes of the reed-blade. Clare, in his "Shepherd's Calendar," thus describes the making and meaning of the knots:

> "When I was young, and went a-weeding wheat,
> We used to make them on our dinner-seat.
> We laid two blades across, and lapt them round,
> Thinking of those we loved; and, if we found
> Them linked together when unlapt again,
> Our loves were true; if not, the wish was vain.
> I've heard old women, who first told it me,
> Vow that a truer token could not be."

Burton notes that, when at his father's house at Lindley, in Leicestershire, he "first observed an amulet of a spider in a nutshell, wrapped in silk, so applied for an ague" by his mother; and his surprise disappeared when he found "this very medicine in Dioscorides, approved by Matthiolus, repeated by Aldrovandus."

Ashmole says, in his "Diary": "I took, early in the morning, a good dose of elixir, and hung three spiders about my neck, and they drove my ague away. *Deo gratias!*"–"Spiders and their webs," says Pettigrew, "have often been recommended for the cure of the ague."

The custom of throwing an old shoe for good luck over or after the bride and bridegroom, upon their leaving the church, or the home of the bride, after the wedding, has of late years been, as it were revived. It is, unquestionably, one of those demonstrations of good wishes which find their way in the commonest modes of expression. But it is not confined to weddings; it extends to all prospective views of good fortune.

It is related that an English cattle dealer desired his wife to "trull her left shoe arter him" when he started for Norwich to buy a lottery ticket. As he drove off on his errand, he looked round to see if she practiced the charm, and consequently he received the shoe in his face, with such force as to black his eyes. He went and bought his ticket, which turned up a prize of £600.

In Tennyson's "Lyrical Monologue" we read:

"For this thou shalt from all things seek
   Marrow of mirth and laughter;
And whereso'er thou move, Good Luck
   Shall throw her old shoe after."

The horseshoe has been, from time immemorial, considered a protection from witchcraft and other ills, and has been nailed at the entrance of dwellings to prevent the entrance of witches.

Butler, in "Hudibras," makes his conjuror chase away evil spirits by the horseshoe, and Gay, in one of his Fables, makes a supposed witch complain:

"The horseshoe's nailed, each threshold's guard."

Nelson, the great English admiral, was of a credulous turn, had great faith in the luck of a horseshoe, and one was nailed to the mast of the ship *Victory*. "Lucky Dr. James" attributed the success of his fever-powder to his finding a horseshoe. When a poor apothecary, he was introduced to Newbery, of St. Paul's Churchyard, to vend the medicine for him. One Sunday morning, as James was on his way to Newbery's country-house at Vauxhall, in passing over Westminster Bridge, seeing a horseshoe lying in the road, and considering it be a sign of good luck, he put the shoe into his pocket. As Newbery was a shrewd man, he became James's agent for the sale of the fever-powder, whilst the doctor ascribed all his success to the horseshoe, which he subsequently adopted as the crest upon his carriage.

Cauls are little membranes found on some children, encompassing the head, when born. This is thought a good omen to the child itself, and many believe that who ever obtains it by purchase will be fortunate and escape dangers. The caul is esteemed an infallible preservative against drowning, and is much sought after by sailors.

The casual putting of the left shoe on the right foot, or the right on the left, was thought in old times to be the forerunner of some unlucky accident. Scott, in his "Discovery of Witchcraft," tells us: "He that receiveth a mischance will consider whether he put not on his shirt wrong side outwards, or his left shoe on his right foot." Thus Butler, in his "Hudibras":

"Augustus, having b' oversight,
Put on his left shoe 'fore his right,
Had like to have been slain that day,
By soldiers mutin'yng for pay."

Similar to this is putting on one stocking with the wrong side outward, without design, though changing it alters the luck, and if you accidently put on any garment wrong side out, and make a wish before changing it, the wish will come true. To arise on the right side is accounted lucky. In the old play of the "Dumb Knight," published 1633, Act. iv., Scene I, Alphonso says:

"Sure I said my prayers, rose on my right side,
Washed my hands and eyes, put on my girdle last;
Sure I met no splay-footed baker,
No hare did cross me, nor no bearded witch,
Nor other ominous sign."

When the nose itches it is a sign that you will have company visit you the same day. So, in Dekker's old play of the "Honest Whore," Bellfront says:

"We shall ha' guests today, I'll lay my little
    maidenhead, my nose itcheth so."

The reply made by her servant, Roger, further informs us that the biting of fleas was a token of the same kind. In Melton's "Astrologaster," No. 31, it is observed "that when a man's nose itcheth it is a sign he shall drink wine," and in No. 32 that, "if your lips itch, it is a sign that you shall kisse somebody."

The nose falling a-bleeding appears, by the following passage from an old play, to have been an omen of bad luck:

"How superstitiously we mind our evils!
The throwing down of salt, or crossing of a hare,
Bleeding at the nose, the stumbling of a horse,
Or singing of a cricket, are of power
To daunt whole man in us."

Washing the hands, says Grose, in the same basin, or with the same water, that another person has washed in, is extremely unlucky, as the parties will infallibly quarrel.

Candle omens are very numerous. Melton, in his "Astrologaster," says: "If a candle burne blue, it is a signe that there is a spirit in the house, or not farre from it." A collection of tallow, says Grose, rising up against the wick of a candle, is styled a winding sheet, and deemed an omen of death in the family.

A spark at the candle, says the same author, denotes that the party opposite to it will shortly receive a letter. A kind of fungus in the candle, observes the same writer, predicts the visit of a stranger from the part of the country nearest the object. Others say it implies the arrival of a parcel.

Dr. Goldsmith, in his "Vicar of Wakefield," speaking of the waking dreams of his hero's daughters, says: "The girls had their omens, too; they saw rings in the candles."

In the "Secret Memoirs of the late Mr. Duncan Campbell," published in London, 1732, the author says: "I have seen people who, after writing a letter, have prognosticated to themselves the ill success of it if by any accident it happened to fall to the ground; others have seemed as impatient and exclaiming against their want of thought if, through haste or forgetfulness, they have chanced to hold it before the fire to dry; but the mistake of a word in it is a sure omen that whatever requests it carries shall be refused."

If two spoons are accidently placed in a cup or saucer at table, it signifies a wedding will soon take place in the family.

To have a picture drop out of its frame, or to have a precious stone or any ornament drop from its setting while wearing or using it, is a bad omen.

Stow, in his "Chronicle," relates that the silver cross which was wont to be carried before Wolsey fell out of its socket, and was like to have knocked out the brains of one of his servants. A very little while after came in a messenger, and arrested the cardinal, before he could get out of the house.

The removal of a long-worn ring from the finger was thought unlucky in Elizabeth's time, for the queen, in her last illness (says Baker), commanded the ring to be filed off her finger, wherewith she was so solemnly at first inaugurated into the kingdom, and since that time had never taken it off; it being grown into the flesh of the finger in such a manner that it could not be drawn off without filing.

There is an omen called "Setting the New Year in," that, if the kindly office is performed by someone with dark hair, good fortune will smile on the household; while it augurs ill if a light-haired person is the first to enter the house in the New Year.

It is a very ancient superstition that all sudden pains of the body, and other sensations which could not naturally be accounted for, were presages of somewhat that was shortly to happen. Shakespeare alludes to this in the following lines from "Macbeth:"

"By the pricking of my thumbs,
Something wicked this way comes."

In olden times the cat sneezing appears to have been considered as a lucky omen to a bride who was to be married the next day.

Small spiders, termed "money spinners," are held by many to prognosticate good luck, if they are not destroyed or injured, or removed from the persons on whom they are first observed. In the "Secret Memoirs" of Mr. Duncan Campbell, in the chapter of omens, we read that "others have thought themselves secure of receiving money if by chance a little spider fell upon their clothes."

It is extremely unlucky, says Grose, to kill a ladybug, a swallow, robin redbreast, or wren. There is a particular distich, he adds, in favor of the robin and wren:

"A robin and a wren
Are God Almighty's cock and hen."

Persons killing any of the above-named birds or insects, or destroying their nests, will infallibly, within the course of the year, break a bone, or meet with some other dreadful misfortune. On the contrary, it is deemed lucky to have swallows build their nests in the eaves of a house, or in the chimneys.

In an old pastoral published in London, 1770, the following occurs:

"I found a robin's nest within our shed,
And in the barn a wren had young one's bred.
I never take away their nest, nor try
To catch the old ones, lest a friend should die,
Dick took a wren's nest from his cottage side,
And ere a twelvemonth past his mother dy'd."

It is deemed very unlucky to hear a screech owl at night. "If an owl," says Bourne, "which is reckoned a most abominable and unlucky bird, send forth its hoarse and dismal voice, it is the omen of the approach of some terrible thing–that some dire calamity and some great misfortune is at hand."

This omen occurs in Chaucer:

"The jealous swan, ayenst hys deth that singeth,
The oule eke, that of deth the bode bringeth."

The following lines occur in the old pastoral by Grose:

"Within my cot, where quiet gave me rest,
Let the dread screech owl build her hated nest,
And from my window o'er the country send
Her midnight screams to bode my latter end."

It has always been considered a very bad omen to have a hare, sow or weasel cross your path when going on a journey or to business. Melton, in his "Astrologaster," says that "it is a very unfortunate thing for a man to meet early in the morning an ill-favored man or woman, a rough-footed hen, a shag-haired dog, or a black cat." Shaw, in his "History of Money," tells us that the ancient Scots much regarded omens in their expeditions; an armed man or a wolf meeting them was a good omen; if a woman, barefoot, crossed the road before them, they seized her and fetched blood from her forehead; if a deer, fox, hare, or any kind of game appeared, and they did not kill it, it was an unlucky omen." We gather from a remarkable book, entitled "The Schoolmaster," published in London, 1583, that in the ages of chivalry it was thought unlucky to meet with a priest if a man was going forth to war or a tournament.

The following superstitions among the Malabrians are related in Phillip's account of them, published in 1717:

"It is interpreted as a very bad sign if a blind man, a Bramin, or a washerwoman meets one on the way; as also when one meets a man with an empty panel, or when one sees an oil-mill, or if a man meets us with his head uncovered, or when one hears a weeping voice, or sees a cat or fox crossing the way, or a dog running on his right hand, or when a poor man or a widow meets us on our way, or when we are called back."

Gaule, in his "Mag-astromancers Posed and Puzzel'd," holds it as a vain observation "to bode good or bad luck from the rising up on the right or left side; from lifting the left leg over the threshold, at first going out of doors; from the meeting of a beggar or a priest the first in the morning; the meeting of a virgin or a harlot first; the running in of a child between two friends; the justling one another at unawares; one treading upon another's toes; to meet one fasting that is lame or defective in any member; to wash in the same water with another."

To comb your hair after dark is also a sign of disappointment.

If a young lady loses her garter, it presages that she has an inconstant lover; therefore, O lady, when thou hast this illaugury, look about thee, and become the happy possessor of two stings to thy bow, or, what is the same thing, two beaus to thy string."

N. B.–Rich or very good-looking young ladies may treat the above with disdain.

If you sing before breakfast, it denotes that you will cry before supper.

To drop a dishcloth, duster, or any cleaning cloth, signifies the arrival of one or more visitors.

If a spider, in weaving his web in some high place, comes downward before your face, you may look for money from some unexpected source.

If you make a rhyme involuntarily, before speaking again make a wish, and it will be fulfilled.

When you sleep in a strange bed, remember your dream and tell it before breakfast. Observing these precautions, the dream will probably come to pass.

To break a needle while making a garment is a sign that the owner will live to wear it out.

If you return after starting a journey, it signifies bad luck.

To remove a cat, with a family when changing residence, will bring bad luck.

If a vacant rocking-chair is rocked violently, the next person who sits in it will be in danger of being ill within the year.

It is a lucky sign to have crickets in the house. Grose says it is held extremely unlucky to kill a cricket, perhaps from the idea of its being a breach of hospitality, this insect taking refuge in houses. The voice of the cricket, says the "Spectator," has struck more terror than the roaring of a lion.

The following line occurs in Dryden's and Lee's Œdipus":

"Owls, ravens, crickets, seem the watch of death."

Melton says that "it is a sign of death to some in that house where crickets have been many years, if on a sudden they foresake the chimney."

It is said that a married person will not get rich until the wedding clothes are worn out. It is also said to be a sign that one will fail to get rich who tries to see work between daylight and dark.

It is a bad omen to postpone a marriage after the time positively appointed.

If your right ear burns or itches, it is a sign that some absent person is speaking well of you; your left ear burning signifies that you are being spoken ill of.

The superstition has become almost universal that the ticking of a little insect called the "death-watch" presages the death of someone in the house.

"How many people have I seen in the most terrible palpitations, for months together, expecting every hour the approach of some calamity, only by a little worm which breeds in an old wainscot, and, endeavoring to eat its way out, makes a noise like the movement of a watch!"–"Secret Memoirs of the late Mr. Duncan Campbell," 1732.

The following witty account of this superstition, by Dean Swift, furnishes us with a charm to avert the omen:

    –"A wood-worm
That lies in old wood, like a hare in her form,
With teeth or with claws it will bite, or will scratch,
And chambermaids christen this worm a death-watch,
Because, like a watch, it always cries click;
Then woe be to those in the house who are sick;
For as sure as a gun they will give up the ghost,
If the maggot cries click, when it scratches the post.
But a kettle of boiling water injected
Infallibly cures the timber affected;
The omen is broken, the danger is over,
The maggot will die, and the sick will recover."

If a knife, scissors, or any sharp-pointed instrument, is dropped, and stands, sticking in the floor, company may be expected.

The right hand itching is a sign that the person will shake hands with a stranger; the left hand itching is a sign that money will be received soon.

If you sing during any meal it is a sign you will soon be disappointed.

To cross a funeral procession is an ill omen.

To find a pearl in an oyster betokens good fortune.

To break a looking-glass betokens a mortality in the family, commonly the master." Bonaparte's (Napoleon I). superstition upon this point is often recorded. "During one of his campaigns in Italy," says M. de Constant, "he broke the glass over Josephine's portrait. He never rested till the return of the courier he forthwith dispatched to assure himself of her safety, so strong was the impression of her death upon his mind."

To find a trefoil, or four-leaved clover, implies good luck; a five-leaved clover, bad luck. Melton, in his "Astrologaster," says that "if a man walking in the fields find any four-leaved grass, he shall, in a small while after, find some good thing."

If four persons cross hands while in the act of shaking hands, it indicates that two of the party will soon be married.

If three unmarried persons having the same Christian name meet at a table, it is a sign that one of the three will be married within a year.

To be startled by a snake is a sign of sickness.

When thirteen persons sit down together at a table, it is

a sign that one of the party will die within a year. Fosbroke, in his "Encyclopaedia of Antiquities," states that "thirteen in company was considered an unlucky number by the ancient Romans;" but he does not give any classical authority for this statement.

There is at Dantzic a clock which at twelve admits, through a door, Christ and the eleven, shutting out Judas, who is admitted at one. But is not the belief older than the clock? The inquiry of Judas may have led him to be considered the thirteenth at the Lord's Supper; and his self-destruction may have given to the number thirteen its fatal association.

I has, however, been explained away by M. Quetelet, in his work on "Probabilities," as follows: "If the probability be required that out of thirteen persons of different ages one of them, at least, shall die within a year, it will be found that the chances are about one to one that one death, at least will occur. This calculation, by means of a false interpretation, has given rise to the prejudice, no less ridiculous, that the danger will be avoided by inviting a greater number of guests, which can only have the effect augmenting the probability of the event so much apprehended."

This belief obtains in Italy and Russia, as well as in England. Moore, in his "Diary," vol ii., p. 206, mentions there being thirteen at dinner one day at Madam Catalain's, when a French countess who lived with her upstairs was sent for to remedy the grievance.

"Lord L (andsdowne) said he had dined once abroad with Count Orloff, and perceived he did not sit down at dinner, but kept walking from chair to chair; he found afterward it was because the Narishken were at table, who, he knew, would rise instantly if they perceived the number thirteen, which Orloff would have made by sitting down himself."

If a dog bays under your window at night, it portends sickness or death.

Shakespeare ranks this among omens. In the play of "Henry VI," he says:

"The Owl shrieked at thy birth; an evil sign!
The night-crow cry'd, aboding luckless time;
Dogs howl'd, and hideous tempests shook down trees."

The howling of dogs, says Grose, is a certain sign that someone of the family will very shortly die.

The following passage is in the "Merry Devil" of Edmonton, 1631:

"I hear the watchful dogs
With hollow howling tell of thy approach."

If you break your shoe-string, look out for your sweetheart, for she will bestow her love upon a stranger

A flake of soot hanging at the bars of the grate denotes the visit of a stranger, like the fungus of a candle, from the part of the country nearest the object.

Dr. Goldsmith, in his "Vicar of Wakefield," among the omens of his hero's daughters, tells us "purses bounded from the fire." In some parts of England the cinders that bound from the fire are carefully examined by old women and children, and, according to their respective forms, are called either "coffins" or "purses;" and consequently, thought to be presages of death or wealth.

A coal, says Grose, in the shape of a coffin, flying out of the fire toward any particular person, betokens their death not far off.

Cowper alludes to this superstition in the following lines in his "Winter Evening":

> "Me oft has fancy, ludicrous and wild,
> Sooth'd with a waking dream of houses, towers.
> Trees, churches, and strange visages express'd
> In the red cinders, while with poring eye
> I gazed, myself creating what I saw.
> Nor less amused have I quiescent watch'd
> The sooty films that play upon the bars,
> Pendulous, and foreboding in the view
> Of superstition, prophesying still,
> Though still deceived, some stranger's near approach."

To drop a slice of bread with the buttered side down, is a sign that a visitor will come hungry.

To eat up all the food which is on the table at tea-time is a sign that the morrow will be a fair day.

In olden times it was not considered a good omen to find money." We have seen superstitious people at the present day keep for luck any piece of money they found, but Greene, in his "Art of Cony-Catching," a very old work, tells us: "'Tis ill lucke to keep found money." Therefore it must be spent. Mason, in his "Anatomie of Sorcerie," 1612, enumerating our superstitions, mentions as one omen of good luck, "if drink be spilled upon a man, or if he find old iron." Hence it is accounted a lucky omen to find a horseshoe.

The ancients thought there was luck in odd numbers. In setting a hen, says Grose, the good women hold it as an indispensable rule to put an odd number of eggs. All sorts of remedies are ordered to be taken three, seven or nine times. Salutes of cannon consist of an odd number. Notwithstanding these opinions in favor of odd numbers, the number thirteen is considered very ominous.

Seven, as an astronomical period, is known to most nations, and has been from times prior to history.

The Hebrews commemorated their seventh day, or seventh week–(Pentecost) the seventh month (commencing their civil year), the seventh year (for fallowing the land), and the seven times seventh year, or jubilee.

The seven-eared wheat is the kind formerly raised in Egypt and Syria, and is often mentioned in the Bible under the name of "corn," which meant then any sort of grain of which bread was made. Pharaoh dreamed of the seven-eared corn.

The following are a few of the many instances of this popular adoption of the number seven: Seven Champions. Seven Churches. Seven Days in a Week. Seven Day's Notice. Seven Dials. Sevenfold. Seven Hills. Seven Penitential Psalms. Seven Senses. Seven Sisters. Seven Sleepers. Seven Sons. Seventh Son of the Seventh Son. Seven Times Seven a Jubilee. Seven Wise Men. Seven Wonders of the World. Seven Years, a change. Seven abominations. The seventh son was formerly considered as endowed with pre-eminent wisdom, and the seventh son of a seventh son is still thought to possess the power of healing disease spontaneously. Finally, perfection is likened to gold seven times purified in the fire.

The influence of the number seven over the life of President Andrew Johnson is both curious and interesting. His name consists of seven letters. At fourteen (twice seven) years of age he became a tailor's apprentice, at which occupation he worked seven years, and gave it up when twenty-one (thrice seven) he became alderman of the city of Greeneville. In the year of 1835 (five times seven) he entered the Legislature of Tennessee. In 1842 (six times seven), he became a member of Congress. Entered the Senate at the age of forty-nine (seven times seven).

On the 7th of March, 1862, he was appointed military Governor of the State of Tennessee, and in 1865, aged fifty-six (eight times seven) years, he became Vice-President of the United States.

A knife is in all countries an unlucky present, and a pair of scissors is equally *malapropos*. It is remarkable that no Arab will take knife or scissors from the hands of any one, as it is considered very unlucky; but they require that the instrument should first be laid upon the ground, when they readily take it up without fear.

It is, says Grose, unlucky to present a knife, scissors, razor, or any sharp or cutting instrument, to one's mistresses, or friend, as they are apt to cut love and friendship. To avoid the ill effects of this, a pin, a penny, or some trifling recompense, must be taken in return. Thus Gay, in his second pastoral of "The Shepherd's Week":

"But, woe is me! such presents luckless prove,
For knives, they tell me, always sever love."

To find a knife or razor denotes ill luck and disappointment to the party.

It is unlucky, says Grose, to lay one's knife and fork crosswise; crosses and misfortunes are likely to follow.

To see a new moon, for the first time, over the left shoulder, is a sign of bad luck; over the right shoulder, good luck.

To have money in the pocket at the time a new moon is first seen is a sign that he person will not be out of money before the next moon.

A strange cat coming to the house is said to bring good luck.

If a bee flies in a window and about a room, it is a sign that a letter is coming from a distance containing news.

If a cock crows upon a doorstep early in the morning, company may be expected during the day.

Sailors are very superstitious; they consider it ominous to whistle on shipboard, or carry a corpse in their vessel. Whistling at sea is supposed to cause increase of the wind, and is, therefore, much disliked by seamen, though sometimes they themselves practice it when there is a dead calm. The common sailors account it very unlucky to lose a water bucket or a mop. Children are deemed lucky to a ship, but clergymen and priests very unlucky.

CHAPTER 13

Weather Omens

If the wind be north, northwest or east, then veer to the northeast, remain there two or three days without rain, and then veer to the south without rain; and if thence it change quickly, though perhaps with a little rain, to the northeast, and remain there–such fine weather will last occasionally for two months.

If there be dry weather with a weak south wind for five, six or seven days, it having previously blown strongly from the same quarter.

If spiders, in spinning their webs, make the terminating filaments long, we may, in proportion to their length, conclude that the weather will be serene, and continue so for ten or twelve days.

If there are no falling stars to be seen on a bright summer's evening, you may look for fine weather.

If there be a change from continued stormy or wet to clear and dry weather, at the time of new or full moon, or a short time before or after, and so remain until the second day of the new or full moon, it is likely to remain fine till the following quarter; and if it change not then, or only for a very short time, it is likely to continue fine and dry for four or five weeks.

If there be a change of weather at the time of the quarters, etc. (under the same circumstances as in preceding paragraph), it will probably last for some time.

Spiders generally alter their webs once in twenty-four hours; if they do this between six and seven in the evening, there will be a fine night; if they alter their web in the morning, a fine day; if they work during rain, expect fine weather; and the more active and busy the spider is, the finer will be the weather.

If near the full moon there be a general mist before sunrise; or if there be a sheep-sky, or white clouds driving to the northwest, it will be fine for some days.

FOR CONTINUED RAINY AND SHOWERY WEATHER

If at sunrise many clouds are seen in the west, and then disappear.

If, before sunrise, the fields be covered with a mist.

If the clouds at sunrise fly to the west.

If at sunrise the sun be surrounded by an iris, or circle of white clouds.

If there be red clouds in the west at sunset, it will be fine; if they have a tint of purple, it will be very fine; or if red, bordered with black in the southeast.

If there be a ring or halo round the sun in bad weather.

If the full moon rise clear.

If there be clouds in the east in the evening.

If the wind change from southeast, south or southwest, through the west to the north, without storm or rain.

If there be a change of damp air into cloudy patches, which get thinner.

If clouds at the same height drive up with the wind, and gradually become thinner, and descend.

If a layer of thin clouds drive up from the northwest under other higher clouds driving more south.

If many gnats are seen in spring, expect a warm autumn.

If gnats fly in compact bodies in the beams of the setting sun, there will be fine weather.

If spiders work in the morning early at their webs, there will be a fine day.

If spider's webs (gossamer), fly in the autumn with a south wind, expect an east wind and fine weather.

If bats flutter and beetles fly about, there will be a fine morrow.

If there be lightning without thunder, after a clear day, there will be a continuance of fair weather.

If the mists vanish rapidly, and do not settle upon the hills.

If a north wind remain steady for two or three days.

If it rain before sunrise, there will be a fine afternoon.

If a white mist, or dew, form in the evening near a river, and spread over the adjoining land, there will be fine weather.

If in the morning a mist rise from over low lands, it will be fine that day.

If owls scream during foul weather, it will change to fair.

If storks and cranes fly high and steadily.

If there be a rainbow during continued wet weather, the rain is passing from us.

If a rainbow disappears suddenly, it will be fair.

If a leech be kept in a glass jar, about three parts filled with water, and placed in a northern aspect, its motions will denote changes in the weather. Thus, if the leech lie curled up at the bottom of the jar, the weather will be fine or frosty; if it be agitated and rise to the surface of the water, there will be rain, wind or snow; if it be much agitated, and creep entirely out of the water, expect thunder. During heavy storms, leeches often die in great numbers.

FOR CONTINUED RAINY AND SHOWERY WEATHER

If there be, within four, five or six days, two or three changes of the wind from the north through the west to the south, without much rain and wind, and thence again through the west to the north with rain and wind, expect continued showery weather.

If the northwest or north wind, during three, four or more days, blow, with rain and wind, or snow, in the winter, and then pass through the west to the south, expect continued rain and showers.

If the garden spiders break and destroy their webs, and creep away.

If the air be unusually clear during rain, or a very heavy sky, provided the moon be not above the horizon.

If continued fine weather change to wet by full or new moon, and remain till the second day, this bad weather will probably last until the next quarter, and not change then, or only slightly, till the next new or full moon; when, if it change not, this bad weather will very probably continue four or five weeks.

If there be change of continued fine weather, etc., by the quarters, etc., (under the same circumstances as in the preceding paragraph), the bad weather may be expected to last some time.

When the sky, in rainy weather, is tinged with sea green, the rain will increase; if with deep blue, it will be showery.

FOR FOUL AND WET WEATHER

If the sun rise pale, or pale red, or even dark blue, there will be rain during the day.

If the clouds at sunrise be red, there will be rain the following.

If at sunrise many dark clouds are seen in the west, and remain, there will be rain on that day.

If the sun rise covered with a dark-spotted cloud; rain the same day.

If in the winter there be a red sky at sunrise; steady rain same day; in summer, showers and wind.

If the sun set in dark, heavy clouds, rain next day;

But if it rain directly, wind the following day.

If the sun set pale or purple, rain or wind the following day.

If the sun set, and there be a very red sky in the east, wind; in the southeast, rain.

If long strips of clouds drive at a slow rate high in the air, and gradually become larger, the sky having been previously clear, there will be wet.

If there be many falling stars on a clear evening, in the summer, there will be thunder.

If there be a change of the wind from the northwest or west, to the southwest or south, or else from the northeast or east, to the southeast or south, wet.

If the sun burn more than usual, or there be a halo round the sun during fine weather, wet.

If it rain and the sun shine, showers.

If the full moon rise pale, wet.

If the full moon rise red, wind.

If the stars appear larger, and closer, and flicker, rain or wind.

If small white clouds, with rough edges be seen together, there will be wind.

Before thunder it often begins to blow.

If there be a fleecy sky, unless driving northwest, wet.

If clouds, at different heights float in different directions.

If an assemblage of large or small clouds spread out, or become thicker and darker.

If clouds suddenly appear in the south.

If the lower clouds drive more from the south than those above.

If there be rain about two hours after sunrise, it will be followed by showers.

If there be a damp fog, or mist, accompanied with wind, wet.

If there be a halo round the moon, in fine weather; and the larger the circle, the nearer the rain.

If the stars above forty-five degrees, especially the North Star, flicker strongly and appear closer than usual, there will be rain.

If the morning be clear and sunny, in summer or autumn, there will be rain.

If the fields in the morning be covered with a heavy, wet fog, it will generally rain within two or three days.

"A rainbow in the morning is the shepherd's warning."

If the leaves of the tree move without any perceptible wind, rain may be expected.

If there be a west and southwest wind in July and December, much rain.

If there be a north wind in April, rain.

If there be an abundance of hoar-frost, rain.

If there be in May a southwest wind, genial showers.

If mists rise and settle on the hill tops, rain.

If the sky, after fine weather, become wavy, with small clouds, rain.

If in winter, the clouds appear fleecy, with a very blue sky, expect snow or cold rain.

If the clouds pass in opposite directions, both currents moving rapidly, expect more rain.

If the wind blow between north and east, or east, with clouds, for some days, and if clouds be then seen driving from the south high up, rain will follow plentifully, sometimes forty-eight hours afterwards. If, after or during the rain, the wind goes to the south or southwest, better weather.

If there be a continuance of rain from the south, it will be scarcely ever succeeded by settled weather before the wind changes, either to the west or some point of the north.

If rain fall during an east wind, it may be expected to last twenty-four hours.

If old and rheumatic people complain of their corns

and joints, and limbs once broken ache at the place of their union.

If the smoke from chimneys blow down; or if soot take fire more readily than usual, or fall down the chimney into the grate, expect rain.

If ditches and drains smell stronger than usual, expect rain; as also if tobacco smoke seems denser and more powerful.

If the marigold continue shut after seven in the evening, rain.

If the convolvulus and chickweed close, there will be rain.

If sheep, rams and goats spring about in the meadow, and fight more than usual.

If asses shake their ears, bray and rub against walls or trees.

If cattle leave off feeding, and chase each other in their pastures.

If cats lick their bodies and wash their faces.

If foxes and dogs howl and bark more than usual; if dogs go sleepy and dull, also if they eat grass.

If swine be restless, and grunt loudly; if they squeak and jerk up their heads, there will be much wind; whence the proverb–"Pigs can see the wind."

If moles cast up hills, rain if through openings in the frozen turn, or through a thin covering of snow, a change to open weather may be expected.

If horses stretch out their necks and sniff the air, and assemble in the corner of a field, with their heads to leeward, rain.

If rats and mice be restless and squeak much.

If peacocks and guinea-fowls scream and turkeys gobble, and if quails make more noise than usual.

If seabirds fly toward land, and land birds to sea.

If the cock crows more than usual, and earlier.

If swallows fly lower than usual.

If the crows make a great deal of noise, and fly around and around.

If water fowl scream more than usual, and plunge into the water.

If birds in general pick their feathers, wash themselves and fly to their nests.

If cranes place their bills under their wings.

If bees remain in their hives, or fly but a short distance from them.

If fish bite more readily, and gambol near the surface of the streams or ponds.

If gnats, flies, etc., bite sharper than usual.

If worms creep out of the ground in great numbers

If frogs and toads croak more than usual.

If the cricket sing louder than usual.

If wood lice run about in great number.

If the owl screech.*

If the sea-anemone shut; and according to the extent it open, so will the weather be fine or less so.

---

*As the owl is most noisy at the change of weather, and as it often happens that patients with lingering diseases die at the change of weather, so the owl, by a mistaken association of ideas, has been said to foretell death.

FOR STORM

If the clouds be of different heights, the sky above being grayish, or dirty blue, with hardly any wind stirring; the wind, however, changing from west to south, or sometimes to southeast, without perceptibly increasing in force.

If there be a clouded sky, and dark clouds driving fast (either with the wind or more from the south), under the higher clouds, violent gusts of wind.

If there be long points, tails, or feathers hanging from thunder or rain clouds, five, six or more degrees above the horizon, with little wind, in summer, thunder may be expected; but the storm will be generally of short duration.

If there be a light-blue sky, with thin, light, flying clouds, whilst the wind goes to the south without much increase in force, or a dirty-blue sky, where no clouds are to be seen, storm.

If the sun be seen double, or more times reflected in the clouds, expect a heavy storm.

If the sun set with a very red sky in the east, expect stormy wind.

If two or three rings be seen round the moon, which are spotted and spread out, expect a storm of long continuance.

If porpoises and whales sport about ships.

If seagulls and other birds fly inland.

Storms are most frequent in December, January and February. In September there are generally one or two storms. If it blow in the day, it generally hushes toward evening; but if it continue blowing then, it may be expected to continue. The vernal equinoctial gales are stronger than the autumnal.

FOR INCREASE OF STORM

If the sky become darker, without much rain, and divide into two layers of clouds, expect sudden gusts of wind.

If the sun or moon be passing through the south or north, the storm having already commenced.

FOR DECREASE OF STORM

The rising or setting of sun or moon, but especially of the moon.

FOR THUNDER AND HEAVY RAIN

If long, horizontal strips appear with two or three edges spreading out at top into feathers, and passing over the middle of other clouds, generally there will be thunder.

If the clouds be uniformly black, or dark gray.

In May and July it thunders most; in May, except thunder with a southwest wind.

If there be northeast or easterly wind in the spring, after a strong increase of heat, and small clouds appear in different parts of the sky; of if the wind change from east to south at the appearance of clouds preceded by heat.

If a morning fog form into clouds, at different heights, which increase in size and drive in layers.

If clouds float at different heights and rates, but generally in opposite directions.

If there be many "falling stars" on a fine summer's eve.

If there be sheet lightning, with a clear sky, on spring, summer and autumn evenings.

If the wind be hushed with sudden heat.

If clover contract its leaves.

If there be thunder in the evening, there will be much rain and showery weather.

FOR THE APPROACH OF THUNDER

If an east wind blow against a dark, heavy sky from the westward, the wind of decreasing in force as the clouds approach.

If the clouds rise and twist in different directions.

If the birds be silent.

If cattle run round and collect together in the meadows.

FOR CONTINUED THUNDER SHOWERS

If there be showery weather, with sunshine, and increase of heat in the spring, a thunder storm may be expected every day, or at least every other day.

ABATEMENT OF THUNDER STORMS

If the air be very dry, with clear, yet cooler weather; or if one or two following days the atmosphere be heavy, with a little damp falling.

With a north wind it seldom thunders; but with a south and southwest wind, often.

FOR COLDER WEATHER

If the wind change to the north and northeast.

If the wind change, in summer only, to the northeast.

If the wind shift to the east in summer only.

If the wind shift from south to southeast in winter.

FOR INCREASE OF WARMTH OR HEAT

If the wind shift round to the south and southwest.

If the wind change from east, northeast or north, to northwest and west, in the winter.

If the wind change to the east, in summer only; especially if from northeast.

If the wind change to southeast, especially in summer.

FOR FROST

If birds of passage arrive early from colder climates.

If the cold increase while it snows, as soon as it begins to freeze.

If the wind blow northeast in winter.

If the ice crack much, expect the frost to continue.

If the mole dig his hole two feet and a half deep, expect a very severe winter; if two feet deep, not so severe; one foot deep, a mild winter.

If waterfowl or sparrows make more noise than usual; also if robins approach nearer houses than usual, frost.

If there be a dark, gray sky, with a south wind.

If there be continued fogs.

If the fire burn unusually fierce and bright in winter, there will be frost and clear weather; if the fire burns dull, expect damp and rain.

It seldom freezes with a west wind; not much with a north; most with a northeast, southeast and sometimes south wind.

FOR THAW

If snow fall in flakes, which increase in size.

If the heat increase in the afternoon, or suddenly before twelve o'clock.

If clouds drive up high from the south, southwest or west.

If it freeze, and the barometer fall twenty or thirty hundredths.

MISCELLANEOUS

If the dew lies plentifully on the grass after a fair day, it is the sign of another. If not, and there is no wind, rain must follow.

A red evening portends fine weather; but if it spread too far upward from the horizon in the evening, and especially morning, it foretells wind or rain, or both.

Against much rain, the clouds grow bigger and increase very fast, especially before thunder.

A haziness in the air, which fades the sun's light, and makes the orb appear whitish, or ill-defined—or at night, if the moon and stars grow dim, and a ring encircles the former, rain will follow.

When the clouds are formed like fleeces, but dense in the middle and bright toward the edges, with the sky bright, they are signs of a frost, with hail, snow or rain.

If clouds form high in air, in thin, white trains, like locks of wool, they portend wind and probably rain.

When a general cloudiness covers the sky, and small black fragments of clouds fly underneath, they are a sure sign of rain and probably it will be lasting.

If the sun's rays appear like Moses' horns—if white at setting or shorn of his rays, or goes down into a bank of clouds in the horizon, bad weather is to be expected.

If the moon look pale and dim, we expect rain; if red, wind; and if of her natural color, with a clear sky, fair weather.

If the moon is rainy throughout, it will be clear at the change, and perhaps the rain return a few days after. If fair throughout, and rain at the change, the fair weather will probably return on the fourth or fifth day.

When the new moon is first seen lying flat on its back, it foretells a drought; if it is partially inclined, sufficiently so that a pail of water might be hung on the lower horn and not spill, it denotes fair weather; if it appears to stand nearly upright, it indicates rain and is called a wet moon.

If a snowstorm begins at a time when the moon is young, the rising of the moon will clear snow away.

If it rains while the sun is shining, it signifies rain on the following day.

A rainbow toward evening is a promise of clear weather, but in the morning it betokens rain.

The first frost of the season appears six weeks after the katydids are first heard.

A fog in February denotes a frost in the following May.

CHAPTER 14

Written on the Palm

The life story written on the palm is easily intelligible by the aid of the following brief, but comprehensive explanation.

Palmistry has ever been the favorite method employed by gypsies for foretelling fortunes, and there can be no doubt about its reliability.

LIFE LINE

The Life Line or Heart Line, is called the Cardiaca, and runs from the inner edge of the hand between the thumb and forefinger nearly at right angles, usually terminating near the outer edge. If it is broad and long, of good color, and with but few crosses, it is a sign of long life. If slender and short, it foretells sickness and a short life. If it is broken it is a sign of great danger of losing your life when arriving in that part of it, counting the end between the thumb and the forefinger as the commencement of life. Where crosses appear on it, they show that you had trouble or are to have trouble. If the crosses are at the end of the line toward its base, it predicts that you had a misfortune, such as losing your father or mother in infancy; and the crosses as they show themselves along the line predict troubles or misfortunes. If this line be thicker than ordinary at its base between the forefinger and thumb, it is a sign you will live to a good old age, and be industrious, frugal and of ample means.

LIVER LINE

The Epatica, or Liver Line, runs from the outside of the hand towards a space between the base of the heart line and the forefinger. If it is well marked and straight, it is a sign of a sound constitution, healthful body, and good fortune generally. If it be short and broken, and goes no further than the hollow of your hand, it foretells sickness and death. If cut at the extreme end by a short intervening line, it predicts poverty in old age. If it winds and turns in its course, it shows that you have a bad liver, and are covetous and depraved, especially if such winding should be near or in any way connect with the middle finger. If it be double, it is a sign some one will leave you a legacy. If crossed near the middle finger, it is a sign of a death when you arrive at that stage of the line–either your own or that of a near relative.

BRAIN LINE

The Cephalica, or Line of the Brain, connects the lines of the Liver and Heart in a triangular form, running from the inside edge of the hand between the thumb and forefinger towards the wrist. If it forms proper triangles with those lines, it is a sign of good-heartedness, wit and courage. If the triangles are out of shape, it augurs an evil-disposed nature in man, and a loose one in woman. If no triangles are formed by this line, it shows the person to be foolish and short-lived. If it is joined at its base by numerous little lines, it foretells a prudent and joyful old age. If, in conjunction with any other line, it turns so as to make the two lines run parallel like the prongs of a fork, it is a sign of riches and honor.

TABLE LINE

Thoralis, or the Table Line, runs from the inside edge of the hand between the thumb and forefinger towards the base of the little finger. If it is pretty straight and unbroken, it is a sign of a strong constitution and firmness of purpose. Sometimes little lines sprout from this one and run between the fingers, or opposite the base of the fingers. If one of these lines terminate at the base of the middle finger it denotes wealth and honors; if at the ring finger, it foretells success in love; if between the middle and ring fingers, it is a sign of sorrow and disappointment; if between the fore and middle fingers, you will some day lose a large sum of money, either by being cheated or by making a bad bargain.

THE DRAGON'S TAIL

Restricta, or the Dragon's Tail, starts from the base of the thumb, near the wrist, and runs up toward the inner edge of the hand across the ham of the thumb. Sometimes it is double, and that is a sign of good fortune, and much riches, particularly when the line toward the hollow of the hand is the most continuous and distinctly marked. Crosses on the Restricta denote tranquility of life in a man, but misfortune and infamy in a woman. If the Restricta extends plainly to the forefinger, it predicts that you will some day live in a foreign country.

SUN'S LINE

The Solis, or Sun's Line, branches down from the forefinger. The Lactea, or Milky Line, comes from the ring finger. The Saturnia, or Line of Saturn, extends from the Heart Line to the middle finger. All these lines, when plainly marked, are favorable auguries of fortune. That of the Sun of brave fortune, of Saturnia, of riches and honors, and the Lactea is a sign of luck in love matters.

MINOR LINES

In addition to the above, there are marks across the thumb and fingers, which also have their signs.

Over thwart lines, that are clear and long underneath the nail and joint of the thumb, confer riches and honor. A line passing from the upper joint of the thumb to the Life Line of the hand threatens a violent death, or danger, by means of some married lady. Lines everywhere dispersed in the lower joint of the thumb describe men that are contentious, and such as rejoice in scolding, etc. A line surrounding the thumb in the middle joint portends that the man shall be hanged. Equal furrows drawn under the lower joint, argue riches and possessions.

On the forefinger, if there are many lines outside the upper joint, they denote inheritance of some kind. Numerous lines generally on the outside of the forefinger denote favor to men and numerous children to women.

The middle finger presenting little gridirons in the joints thereof, plainly declares an unhappy and melancholy wit, but if equal lines, it manifests fortune by digging gold or working in metals. A star there presages a violent death by drowning, suffocation, or hanging. If a cross line be extended from the root thereof upward, through the whole finger into the end of the last joint, it argues folly and madness.

On the ring finger, a line rising from the base and ascending by a right track through the joints thereof, shows a noble frame. Equal lines in the first joint demonstrate honors and riches. Over thwart lines, the enmity of great men. But if these lines shall seem to be interested, it is the better, because they argue impediments.

Adverse or parallel lines on the last joint of the little finger shows perpetual inconstancy. Some persons predict the number of wives from the little lines on the outmost part of the hand, at the base of this finger, and I have often observed these signs come true; but yet I will have often observed these signs come true; but yet I will not confirm anything in this respect, because it properly appertains to Venus and her disposition. If this finger is not long enough to touch the last joint of the ring finger, it signifies that you will get a wife imperious in all things.

CHAPTER 15

Physiognomy

Physiognomy, or the Features of the Head and Face, teaches us to judge of the character of a person and of evens connected with his destiny from the shape, color and expression of his features. If my fair readers would like to know how many husbands they are to have, they have only to knit their eyebrows closely together, and count the folds of the skin formed by this movement.

If they wish to see how many years they have to live, let them elevate their brows as much as possible, and then count the cross folds in the forehead. Subtract the number found from one hundred, and the remainder is the number of the years which it is allotted you to pass upon this earth.

THE HEAD

A symmetrical head should be so shaped that the top of the ear is precisely in the center of the space from the most prominent point of the forehead to that on the back side of the head. A head of this shape shows a well-balanced disposition; and the person owning it has enough animal energy in the rear to keep in play the intellectual faculties in front. Such people, if they have the right shaped head in other respects, are generally intelligent, industrious and thrifty. A person with a full brain in front, and little or no prominence of the head behind the ears, may be smart enough, but is never active or energetic. There are a great many talented people with this peculiarity of brain. They have all the necessary qualifications to make them great geniuses, but lack of animal energy. A person whose head is prominent in the center of his forehead always has a good memory; and if his eyes bulge out large and round, he will make an excellent public speaker or writer. One whose eyebrows nearest the root of the nose are very prominent has great perceptive faculties, a quick understanding, etc. A person whose forehead is wide from one side to the other, and swells out with a prominence on each side, generally has original ideas, and seldom imitates anybody else. If the prominence extends back toward the top of the ear, he is undoubtedly an original wit, and probably a poet. Many people imagine that a high forehead is always a mark of intellect. It is a popular error. I have known inveterate rogues and thieves to have high and prominent foreheads. It is the shape of the foreheads. The moral faculty are developed on the top of the head. A person with prominent swellings of the brain from forehead to crown you may judge to be benevolent, conscientious, and possessing much self-respect and dignity. The selfish propensities are at the sides of the head, such as caution, secrecy, and love of money and power. A man may have a tolerable prominent head on top, very fair mental faculties in front, with pretty good energy in the rear, and yet if he has a predominance of these side bumps, particularly those of secretiveness and acquisitiveness behind the ear, he will probably be a genteel rogue or swindler. The low and sneaking thieves have the side bumps without much development of the intellectual or moral ones as above described. If you see a person with a prominent swelling on the back point of his head, he will be fond of children. If any one has two prominent swellings at the base of the brain behind each ear, he or she will be fond of the opposite sex. A vain man or woman will have a swelling on the crown of the head, etc. As we do not intend to give a treatise on phrenology, but merely a glance at character from the general shape of the head, it is perhaps unnecessary to say more than that a long head from front to rear, if well balanced, as described above, indicates energy and talent, while a round one, or a bullet head, shows the owners of it to be a person of only ordinary capacity.

THE HAIR

Thick and straight black hair, fine and glossy, on man or woman, is a sign that they are of kind disposition, but resolute, not violent in love, but usually true and faithful. If the same kind of hair be curly, it shows a quick and obstinate temper, more amorous, and less firm in purpose. If the hair be coarse and straight, they will be licentious, and probably unprincipled and improvident.

Thick, straight and glossy fine brown hair shows a robust constitution, one who is energetic, obstinate and eager in the pursuits of life; fond of the opposite sex, and if a woman, steady and true in her attachments. Such people are usually long lived, unless afflicted with some constitutional or hereditary disease. If the hair be coarse and wiry, it shows great determination of character in some and dishonesty in others. If it be curly or kinky, it detracts a good deal from most of the qualities above mentioned, showing a weakness of character, though not a lack of natural ingenuity and ability. In selecting a friend, choose one with fine, silky hair that does not curl, and grows thick on the head.

Light brown or fair hair, when it grows thick and fine shows a gentle disposition, mild manners, a good and generous heart, and generally a person of first-rate qualities. If thin and fine, the same traits of character, though not so marked, and perhaps interspersed with faults. If the hair is curly and kinky, it shows a wavering and unsettled disposition. If coarse and wiry, you may be sure the person is unreliable and dissembling, if not actually dishonest.

Red hair, when fine, thick and glossy, frequently covers persons of good feelings and intentions; but as a general rule they are cunning and suspicious, though perhaps not always treacherous. I speak of the undoubted red. Shades of reddish brown may make a good deal of difference. But I have never found a person with genuine red hair whose frankness of character could be relied on. If the hair be fine and curly, it makes little difference; but if coarse and kinky, you may suspect the person to be anything except one in whom you can place confidence. Straight and coarse red hair is better than curly or kinky red, though either is bad enough to prognosticate character upon. There are exceptions, of course, because some men and women with red hair who do not possess the sandy, thin-skin and white eyebrow complexion. These are people whose hair should be a reddish brown to which their disposition corresponds. Some children have red hair, and their hair turns brown as they grow older. These are not, properly speaking red-headed people. Some genuine red heads train themselves to be very good men and women, but a good many more are selfish and heartless, if not unprincipled. Ladies with red hair are usually great talkers and tattlers.

THE EYEBROWS

Thick and very hairy eyebrows, with long hairs sticking out, shows a person to have a gloomy and dissatisfied mind, to be selfish and greedy in disposition, insincere in friendships and given to excesses of some kind.

Full and even eyebrows show an agreeable temper, sound understanding and good wit. Such persons are generous and sincere and have few faults of character.

Small, thin eyebrows show the person to be irresolute, weak-minded and fickle, but, nevertheless, he (or she) may be industrious, good-tempered and generous. Such persons are fond of praise and are generally kind-hearted.

If the eyebrow is thick toward the nose, and goes off suddenly very thin, ending in a point, the person usually be surly and selfish, fretful and disagreeable in manners, though perhaps not bad-hearted.

THE EYES

Persons with large and bright eyes are usually candid, generous and just. This is the rule, but there are exceptions, particularly among those who have dark hazel or black eyes.

A small, prominent and bright eye shows a quick wit, sound constitution and a warm and generous heart, but a jealous disposition in love affairs. People with such eyes are usually fortunate in their undertakings.

An eye sunk in the head shows the person to be one of strong common sense and great perception, but of a jealous and suspicious nature. Some people with this peculiarity of the eyes are cunning, deceitful, lascivious and treacherous;

but, as a general rule, if they possess such propensities, they govern themselves so as not to disclose them to the world.

People who squint are usually penurious and selfish; but are often strict and honorable in their dealings.

A penetrating black eye shows a person of intellect and wit, but improvident. A snaky and wicked-looking black eye usually belongs to a smart and talented rogue, a seducer, or a treacherous villain.

A speaking hazel eye shows a frank, frolicsome and sometimes mischievous person, of good understanding and amorous propensities.

A mild blue eye generally accompanies amiability of character and belongs to a credulous, confiding and gentle person. Such a person usually has a good memory, is not over liberal with money, and cares but little for the opposite sex.

An inexpressive blue eye, or bird's-egg eye, shows the person to be credulous, foolish, treacherous and often dishonest. You will see hosts of people with eyes of this description—some of them having black hair and black eyebrows and eyelashes. Very few of them are to be trusted at all, and many are kept in curb solely by their extreme caution and superstitious fears of consequences.

A gray eye generally denotes cruelty and indifference to others, though many persons with bright and intelligent gray eyes are good sort of people. It is safer to trust a speaking black eye or a mild blue eye than any gray one. Gray-eyed people are generally smart and industrious.

A wall-eye denotes selfishness, deceit, and a reckless disregard of the opinion of the world. This kind of eye makes very good rogues.

A saucer-eye shows a person who is apt to find fault with and be suspicious of everybody.

Eyes of any color that swell out and look intelligent and speaking show that the person is capable of being a great writer or public speaker. If on a woman, she is probably a great talker and an agreeable companion.

THE NOSE

A person with a sharp nose, whether man or woman, is always shrewish. One with a flat, fleshy, spreading nose is generally vain and silly. A turn-up nose usually predicts smartness and honesty, though there are doubtless rogues with such noses. A very large nose which bulges out in the center shows a lack of intellect where the person's face is small; but such a nose on a large face predicts that the owner of it is brave, generous, clearheaded and intellectual. A bottle-nose, or one that swells out and turns down on the end, shows the person to be either shiftless or unprincipled, or perhaps both. A hook nose is a sign of a keen and energetic person, but one of little principle, selfish and with a bad heart. A Grecian nose generally belongs to a person of good intellect and understanding, and usually honest, upright and generous. A nose with a straight ridge and square on the end is a sign that the person owning it is penurious and industrious, but fair and honest in his dealings. Persons with large nostrils are generally smarter and more energetic than those with small ones.

THE FINGERNAILS

Long, narrow fingernails predict a death at the middle age. If the nails grow down on the side into the flesh, it foretells that your health will not be good. If the color of the nails is very pale, it is a sign of sickness. Round fingernails that are perfect and of a delicate pink color show a robust constitution and probably longevity. If they are too white, it is a sign that your liver is affected in a way that may cut your life short. Short and squatty nails, if of a pink color, are not so certain an index of old age as round ones. Nails with ridges in them, and out of the true shape, predict death by fever. White spots on the nails denote good or bad luck, according to position. If in the center of the little finger, it is a sign you will receive a present; if on the ring finger, you can kiss a pretty girl without making her angry; if on the middle finger, you will probably lose something. On the forefinger or thumb, shows that you will soon either receive or pay some money.

LENGTH OF LIFE

Persons with good and very strong teeth generally live to be old. If the lines in your hands are strongly marked and of good pink color, it is a sign you will live to a good old age. Those of middle stature, with a full chest, that is, a chest thick through from breastbone to back, are usually long lived.

GENERAL PHYSIOLOGICAL CHARACTERISTICS

Short life may be inferred from a thick tongue; the appearance of grinders before the age of puberty, thin, straggling and uneven teeth, confused lines in the hand, of a quick but small growth.

A good genius may be expected from a thin skin, middle stature, blue, bright eyes, fair complexion, straight, pretty strong hair, an affable respect, the eyebrows joined, moderation in mirth, an open cheerful countenance, and the temples a little concave.

A dunce may be known by a swollen neck, plump arms, sides and loins, a round head, concave behind, a large fleshy forehead, pale eyes, a dull, heavy look, small joints, snuffing nostrils, and a proneness to laughter, little hands, an ill-proportioned head, either too big or too little, short fingers and thick legs.

Prudence is generally distinguished by a head which is flat on the sides, a broad, square forehead, a little concave in the middle, a soft voice, a large chest, a thin hair, light eyes, either blue, brown or black eyes, and an aquiline nose.

A good memory is commonly attached to those persons who are smaller, yet better formed in the upper than the lower parts, not fat, but fleshy, of a fair, delicate skin, with the poll of the head uncovered, crooked nose, teeth thick set, large ears, with plenty of cartilage.

A bad memory is observable in persons who are larger in their superior than inferior parts, fleshy, though dry and bald.

A good imagination and thoughtful disposition is distinguished by a large prominent forehead, a fixed and attentive look, slow respiration and an inclination of the head.

A good sight is enjoyed by those persons who have generally black, thick, straight eyelashes, large, bushy eyebrows, concave eyes, contracted as it were inward.

Short-sighted people have a stern, earnest look, small, short eyebrows, large pupils and prominent eyes.

Sense of hearing: Those who possess the same in perfection have ears well furnished with gristle, well channeled and hairy.

The sense of smelling is most perfect in those who have large noses, descending very near the mouth, neither too moist nor too dry.

A nice faculty of tasting is peculiar to such as have a spongy, porous, soft tongue, well moistened with saliva, yet not too moist.

Delicacy in the touch belongs to those who have a soft skin, sensible nerves, and nervous sinews, moderately warm and dry.

Timorousness resides where we find a concave neck, pale color, weak, winking eyes, soft hair, smooth, plump breast, shrill, tremulous voice, small mouth, thin lips, broad, thin hands and small, shambling feet.

Melancholy is denoted by a wrinkled countenance, dejected eyes, meeting eyebrows, slow pace, fixed look and deliberate respiration.

An amorous disposition may be known by a fair, slender face, a redundancy of hair, rough temples, broad forehead, moist, shining eyes, wide nostrils, narrow shoulders, hairy hands and arms, well-shaped legs.

Envy appears with a wrinkled forehead, frowning, dejected and squinting look, a pale, melancholy countenance and a dry, rough skin.

Intrepidity often resides in a small body, with red curled hair, ruddy countenance, frowning eyebrows, arched and meeting; eyes, blue and yellowish; large mouth, and red lines in the hand.

Gentleness and complacency may be distinguished by a soft and moist palm, frequency of shutting the eyes, soft movement, slow speech, soft, straight and light-colored hair.

Bashfulness may be discovered by moist eyes, never wide open, eyebrows frequently lowered, blushing cheeks, moderate pace, slow and submissive speech, and bent body.

Temperance or sobriety is accompanied with an equal respiration, a moderate-sized mouth, smooth temples, eyes of an ordinary size, and a short, flat body.

Strength of mind is signified by light, curled hair, a small body, shining eyes, but a little depressed; a grave, intense voice, bushy beard, large, broad back and shoulders.

Pride stands confessed with arched eyebrows, a large, prominent mouth, a broad chest, a slow pace, erected head, shrugging shoulders and staring eyes.

Loquacity may be expected from a bushy beard, broad fingers, pointed tongue, eyes of a ruddy hue, a large, prominent upper lip and a sharp-pointed nose.

Perverseness may be dreaded when we perceive a high forehead, firm, short, thick, immovable neck, quick speech, immoderate laughter, fiery eyes, and short, fleshy hands and fingers.

Of the face.–A lean face is an indication of a wise man; the face plain and fat denotes a person addicted to strife; the face without any rising and swelling indicates a penurious person; a sad face sometimes denotes foolishness, and at other times wisdom; a fat face indicates to be inclined to untruth; a round face signifies folly; a well-proportioned face indicates a person to have virtuous qualities.

Of the forehead.–A large forehead shows a liberal man, but the forehead narrow denotes a foolish person; a long forehead shows one apt to learn; a high forehead, swelling and round, is a sign of a crafty man and a coward; a forehead full of wrinkles shows a man to be envious and crafty.

A pair of eyes which look every one cheerfully and frankly in the face, with an air of simple joy and unaffected innocence, yet, when surprised, droops to the ground, with a certain sly bashfulness, or, when offended by another's glance, turns aside, blushing and confused, such a pair of eyes indicate an amiable character, a faithful heart, a sound understanding and a pure soul. A being with such a pair of eyes we cannot help loving, let the eyes be black, brown, blue, gray, green or yellow, let the nose be stumpy and the features ill-shaped, no one can help regarding their possessor with a feeling of hearty kindness and good will, if not with actual love.

New Falcon Publications
**Publisher of Controversial Books and CDs
Invites You to Visit Our Website:
http://www.newfalcon.com**

At the Falcon website you can:

- Browse the online catalog of all our great titles, including books by Robert Anton Wilson, Christopher S. Hyatt, Israel Regardie, Aleister Crowley, Timothy Leary, Osho, Lon Milo DuQuette and many more
- Find out what's available and what's out of stock
- Get special discounts
- Order our titles through our secure online server
- Find products not available anywhere else including:
    - One of a kind and limited availability products
    - Special packages
    - Special pricing
- And much, much more

Get online today at http://www.newfalcon.com